GANGOFFOUR
DAMAGED GODS

to Alice

Saw this A thought
you might like it

love
Shep

GANGOFFOUR

DAMAGED GODS

A BIOGRAPHY BY PAUL LESTER

OMNIBUS PRESS
LONDON / NEW YORK / PARIS / SYDNEY / COPENHAGEN / BERLIN / MADRID / TOKYO

CONTENTS

To Ben, Ethan and Talia Lester, the youngest and keenest Gang Of Four fans of them all, and to Beryl and Jeffrey Lester, probably the oldest.

INTRODUCTION

Why a Gang Of Four book, and why now? Well, astonishing as it may seem considering their impact and influence, there has never been a Gang Of Four book. So the question might just as easily be: why wouldn't you write a Gang Of Four book? After all, they have been cited as a key inspiration by some of the biggest bands on the planet, from R.E.M. – whose Michael Stipe has admitted, "Gang Of Four knew how to swing. I stole a lot from them" – to The Red Hot Chili Peppers, whose bassist Flea has said, "Gang Of Four were the first rock band I could truly relate to… These Limeys rocked my world." The late Michael Hutchence of INXS declared, "They took no prisoners. It was art meets the devil via James Brown"; even U2's Bono has been heard to mutter something semi-comprehensible about the band's "hard, angular, bold" sound and their "corporation of common sense, a smart bomb of text that had me 'at home feeling like a typist.'"

It could reasonably be argued that, among certain rock musicians, especially the ones who formed in the wake of the late-Seventies post-punk era, Gang Of Four mean as much as The Velvet Underground did to a previous generation. They may not have sold that many records, but they sold to the right people: everyone who heard them went right out and formed a band. In Britain, they pioneered the idea of the white rock band getting funky, making it possible for everyone from A Certain Ratio to Franz Ferdinand to make their dark dance music, their funk noir, their death disco. And in America, where they possibly mean even more and had an even greater impact, Gang Of Four are the third most influential punk-period rock band after The Sex Pistols and The Clash, paving the way for hordes of funked-up metal bands: Rage Against the Machine, Korn, Limp Bizkit and the rest would, as one journalist recently put it, "be unimaginable without the territory that Gang Of Four fearlessly staked out in a bold, visionary stance that few bands could have taken."

And why now? First, because it's 30 years since the release of Gang Of Four's epochal debut single, the 'Damaged Goods EP', and so it's an opportunity for a neat anniversary celebration. And second because, for the last five years, since the emergence of the new indie-funk brigade from both sides of the Atlantic – Franz Ferdinand, The Rapture, Bloc Party, Futureheads – Gang Of Four's name has been dropped so many times it's in danger of being worn out, and yet nobody really knows their story. Who were the Gang Of Four? How did they get to do what they did, and make the changes to music that they did? To what extent were they, in real life, the socialist, even neo-Marxist, firebrands that their lyrics and interviews suggested? What was it in their words and music that meant so much to the generation of British musicians who came of age in the early Eighties, and connected so viscerally with some of the most famous American musicians of the last two decades, including the young Kurt Cobain and Dave Grohl of Nirvana, musicians thousands of miles removed from Gang Of Four's own experiences growing up in recession-ravaged Britain? What happened to the four members of the band? And what is it about the dynamic between them that means they probably won't ever be able to capitalise on the rapturous acclaim they received when they reformed in 2005 for a series of live performances across the globe?

Over the next few hundred pages, those four players – guitarist

Andy Gill, vocalist Jon King, bassist Dave Allen and drummer Hugo Burnham – will explain in forensic detail what it was in their backgrounds that made them make the music and write the words that they did, and what it was in their individual make-ups that would make the band's story so rife with friction and fallouts that they would never achieve the commercial success they deserved, even if their songs, as fiercely intelligent as they were funkily insidious, did make you wonder whether they knew the answers to those questions all along.

Personally, I've been listening to Gang Of Four for most of my adult life, so it made sense for me to write the book. In fact, I lost my virginity to Gang Of Four. I don't mean in that airy-fairy way about losing one's metaphorical virginity to music – i.e. that theirs was the first rock music I fell in love with. No, I mean I literally lost my virginity to them: my very first attempt at sexual union took place one summer evening in 1980 in a front room in Kenton, North-West London, with a girl called Michelle, as the band's debut album, *Entertainment!,* blasted away in the background and Andy Gill's drily propulsive guitar scythed its way through the still night air. Ironic? Perhaps. Because here were songs that shone a bright light on, and dissected with a brutal lack of concern for the niceties of love and romance, cold couplings and contracts between the sexes, soundtracking my very own anxious teenage congress. "Fornication makes you happy," as Jon King, as drily as his partner, intoned the lyrics to 'Natural's Not In It', offering such bald, bold insights into the nature of interpersonal relations in the wider economic and societal context that they made me squirm even more than I was already squirming. By the time the needle hit 'Damaged Goods' and the bit about, "Sometimes I'm thinking that I love you/But I know it's only lust/Your kiss so sweet/Your sweat so sour... Heated couplings in the sun (Or is that untrue?)/Colder couplings in the night (Never saw your body)...", I started wondering if I should have put on Marvin Gaye's *Let's Get It On* instead. But that would have been too obvious, and Gang Of Four, more than anything else, were always about challenging the obvious, forcing the listener to question his or her every move and decision and the motives behind them. Maybe Barry White's *Stone Gon'*, then...

CHAPTER 1

IN THE BEGINNING

"We actually weren't a gang at all. We didn't have that Clash-style Last Gang In Town mentality. We were very bonded for a long time but we had very separate lives once we got off the plane back at Heathrow. It wasn't like we couldn't live without each other. But for a time we were very close." – Dave Allen

Andy Gill was the son of a civil engineer, who became a lecturer, and a part-time teacher mother. He was born on January 1, 1956, in Sevenoaks in Kent. His father left the family when he was 10 years old.

"I'm sure it did have an impact on some of the ideas I would later have for Gang Of Four," admits the man who became GOF guitarist. "It made me think about family and relationships and the roles people play in the family, which are constants throughout Gang Of Four."

Gill attended the Sevenoaks School, a half-Direct Grant and half-private school with some boarders, which had to allow in 700 children annually via the 11-plus system. This is how he and Jon King, born in June the previous year, found their way there from the local primary school.

When he arrived at Sevenoaks in 1967, Gill was in the year

below King, although at the end of his first grade there he skipped a grade and went straight into the third year with King. He says he found it strange to suddenly be in classes alongside pupils older than him.

"Somebody thought I was quite clever but beyond that I don't know why it happened," he says. "I was convinced I was totally ill-equipped to do English or anything arty. I was sure I was a scientist: I was good at biology and maths, although I also liked ancient history."

It was while he was still at primary school that Gill discovered rock'n'roll: the first record he remembers making an impression on him was '(I Can't Get No) Satisfaction' by The Rolling Stones.

"I had it on a permanent loop, and I would march to and from school to it," he recalls. "It was perfect. What an unbelievable riff. I liked the fact that it was so upfront, the stripped-down basicness of it, with no attempt at a tune at all. I was also very interested in *Sgt Pepper*, although I liked the Stones much more than The Beatles. And The Kinks were great."

Gill can recall the day he first met King at secondary school – they were 13 and 14 respectively, and sneaking a crafty fag behind the bike sheds. After that, they became good friends, and they would hang out either at each other's houses, listening to and talking about music, or at school, in the art department. It became a meeting point for the school's junior radicals.

"Looking back," says Gill, "the combination of a certain Sixties cultural and political openness, the events of the time, and a certain amount of pointless repression made the school experience quite a fertile one for left-leaning and oppositional types at the beginning of the Seventies.

"We gravitated to the art department," he explains, "where we had this brilliant teacher called Bob White, who was Mark White from The Mekons' dad. He had this little world going on. He would speak to us like intelligent human beings, about things like Jackson Pollock. It was the first time we had adult conversations

2

about this stuff, on the same level as the teacher, rather than with you as the pupil and him as the authoritarian, reprimanding figure."

Around the turn of the decade, Gill and King formed a band, and they would play gigs at school, village halls or local parties. On one occasion they played a set at the school ball – "somewhat to the horror of the deputy head," according to Gill. They didn't play, as might be expected given the period, progressive rock or glam but what Gill describes as "made-up, riff-based, reggaefied music", with his brother on drums.

"He was always playing stuff," Gill recalls. "My mother put up with a lot. I used to come home at 4.30pm and play my brother's drum kit for 45 minutes. And then he would come and play for God knows how long. My mother would put up with one and a half hours of fucking racket."

Gill made his own guitar, an orange one, using wood and some fret wire. As for guitar heroes, Jimi Hendrix was his "first major love", way above Jeff Beck, Jimmy Page and Eric Clapton, although he quite liked Cream.

"When I was 13 I had a poster of Hendrix on my wall," he recalls. "The day he died, the Sellotape gave way and the poster fell down, although I imagine a lot of people will have similar memories."

Then he discovered Bob Dylan and The Velvet Underground, whose poetic musings and monotone drone-rock, respectively, conceivably influenced his and King's next musical venture, a duo called The Bourgeois Brothers, formed when they were about 16. "It was a bit shambolic and tongue in cheek – we only did two or three gigs," he recalls. "I suspect the name was Jon's idea." Had King, with his working-class credentials, used the word "bourgeois" as a way of mocking his middle-class friend? "I can't remember," says Gill. "He called me lots of things!"

In 1972, Gill began his A-level courses. Because he "had no clue" what he was supposed to be doing, he took maths for three months, biology for three months and French for a further three months.

"I was lost at sea," he says. "I didn't know what I was doing. So I thought, 'What the hell? I'll do geography, economics and physics.' At that time I was being encouraged to do art A level. It was the life I was looking for – I was hanging about the art room a lot, doing photography and bits for fun. Bob [White] said, 'Do what you want.' So I did art A level and got an 'A', although I had to stay on at school for an extra year so I could retake economics and physics. Eventually I got two 'Bs.'"

By the time Gill got to Leeds University in September 1974, where he studied fine art with a subsidiary course in Shakespeare, Jon King had already been there for a year. Gill immediately began thinking about forming another band, one that would combine his twin loves: black rhythm and white noise. "I didn't want to just do funk or reggae, nor did I want to do post-Velvets noise music. I loved them both, but they seemed to belong to different worlds. I wanted to find a middle way."

★   ★   ★

Jon King was born in June 1955 and, although he grew up near Andy Gill, the pair didn't meet until they got to Sevenoaks School. His father was an electrician and his mother a house-wife.

"We were hard up but we did all right," says King. "We lived in a village near Sevenoaks called Kemsing. It was a tiny place, but my parents had lived in a slum off the Old Kent Road and, in the early Fifties, they moved people out via this 'self-build' scheme. So my father and a lot of other skilled working men built the whole road [in Kemsing]. The plasterer, the plumber, the electrician – they all built the road of houses that my mum still lives in.

"It was a very Fifties idea, to get working-class families out of what were then bomb sites – I used to play in a bomb site when I was a kid on the way to see my grandmother; I'd play in the bombed-out building next door to her house. And it was still there in '61/'62. It was great fun."

This all gives the lie to the idea that Dave Allen was the only working-class member of Gang Of Four, that Jon King was a sort of educated, middle-class Johnny Rotten. "No," he says, "I was just really lucky. I'd gone to a normal primary school – I passed the 11-plus, and then I got a place at the local public school, which had a Direct Grant system for entry – they allowed 30 high-scoring kids a year to go into the school funded by the local authority.

"I'm middle-class now but I had a very strong sense that I was working-class. Yes, I'd been to this very privileged school as a result of the strange Direct Grant system, but I was very, very aware of coming from a working-class background."

Surprisingly, given the cerebral nature of his lyrics for Gang Of Four, King's childhood was quite culturally bereft. "My dad left school at 13," he says. "The telly was on the whole time but we didn't have a book in the house. We were, you know, 'Don't talk at the dinner table.' So, no, I wasn't reading *Das Kapital* at the age of 10. We didn't even have a record player. Actually, my parents did have one, but it only played 78s."

Because of the lack of facilities at home, King's first exposure to rock'n'roll happened at school. Aged 11, he would go into the art department where the sixth formers had a record player and they could play whatever they liked – this was 1966/'67. So they played Bob Dylan's *Blonde On Blonde* and *Highway 61 Revisited* endlessly, as well as early Hendrix and Cream. But it was Dylan who had the most profound impact.

King heard Dylan virtually in "real time", some of the older boys at school acquiring copies of his seminal mid-Sixties albums on their release. King had his mind blown as powerfully as Gill did during his first exposure to the Stones.

"When I first heard *Highway 61 Revisited*, the title track amazed me – he didn't sound like anyone I'd ever heard and the lyrics weren't like anything I'd ever heard, either," recalls King. "He didn't sing particularly in tune. They didn't sound like 'pop songs'. I used to hate Beatles music: 'She loves you, yeah, yeah, yeah' – stuff like that. Then they came out with *Rubber Soul* and *Revolver*, which I heard in real time, and I changed my mind."

King's change of attitude towards the Fab Four was perhaps encouraged by their visit, one strange day, to Sevenoaks, during his first year at school. "I ran into The Beatles," recalls King. "I actually, physically, ran into them at the age of 11. For whatever reason, they were building a dining block at the school and, because I had terrible food at home, I used to love school dinners – we used to have boiled mince and boiled onions [at home] whereas at school we had a proper meal. Anyway, we had to go down to this local cinema – they used to do a meals-on-wheels type thing. There was a lot of bullying at the school and if you were small, as you are when you're 11, and by the time you got to the front of the queue you often didn't get any lunch because the bigger boys would have pushed in front and eaten it all.

"So one day I was running really fast to get served before I got pushed out of the way, and me and my two mates ran into these three blokes – who turned out to be John Lennon, George Harrison and Paul McCartney – in Sevenoaks high street. So we looked up and there were the most famous people in the world. And I thought, 'Do I keep running for lunch, or do I stay and try and get The Beatles' autographs?' I thought, 'Bollocks to that' and went for the food option! They had just left Sevenoaks' antique shop, where I heard afterwards that John Lennon had bought a little fly poster that had on it the words, 'For the benefit of Mr Kite there will be a show tonight.' They'd been filming a video for 'Strawberry Fields Forever' in Knowle Park, which surrounded our school."

Notwithstanding his brush with The Beatles, King's favourite rocker remained Dylan: for the Gang Of Four lyricist, *Blonde On Blonde* and *Highway 61 Revisited* were "lyrically two of the most astounding things ever invented", offering escape from the daily grind and pointers towards a less accepting future.

"He was artistically and politically radical, and his records suggested you didn't have to lead a tedious life where you agreed with whatever you get given," says King. His father – who died at 49 from cancer of the colon, "that classic working-class disease, as a result of bad food, basically" – had similar ambitions for his son.

"He always said he didn't want me to work with my hands because it hadn't done him much good – although I don't want to give the impression that we weren't happy, because we were."

Happy, but starved of artistic stimuli. As King puts it, going to Sevenoaks School, which his mother chose because it was the shortest journey from his home (his two brothers attended the local secondary modern because they failed the 11-plus), saved him from a life of tedium, despite the straw hats the pupils had to wear and the fact they had to attend six days a week.

"At home I didn't have a bedroom of my own: I shared one right up to the age of 18 with my brother. I'm making it sound grim – it was actually fun sometimes – but school was brilliant for me," he contends. "I left in the morning and often didn't come home till seven or eight at night. I was from a normal, working-class background, going to a school with very rich kids in it. We never had any money so I never went on a school trip. But it was amazing being exposed to books for the first time."

Even more exciting was the school's art department, run by the inspirational Bob White, where King and Gill would meet along with like minds from the same year group. Many of them went on to become successful in the arts and media, including Adam Curtis, who produced programmes about the Freuds and *Pandora's Box*, the one about Al Qaeda that won several BAFTAs for BBC2; Paul Greengrass, the director of the *Bourne Identity* films; King and Gill; and Kevin Lycett, Tom Greenhalgh and Mark White, who later formed The Mekons. "We were all quite intense and obsessive about what we did there," King recalls. "It was quite a crew."

The school's art department in the late Sixties provided the ideal time and place for King to develop an interest in radical politics, the sort of playful situationist ideas he would pursue in Gang Of Four.

"I got really, really interested in what was going on and what had gone on in Paris," he says. "I was really interested in the revolution in France. I thought it looked fantastic, all these hot girls and blokes throwing bricks at coppers and being clever and funny. I loved all those situationist things. There was a great poster of the time: 'Je sais que je vous exploit mais je ne le fais expresse', which meant, 'I know I'm exploiting you but I'm not doing it on purpose' – I thought this was fantastic, and it proved a big influence on our sleeve for 'Damaged Goods'.

"I thought situationism was great, all those things like, 'Be reasonable, demand the impossible', which were hilariously pretentious but funny. I liked the idea of taking things and turning them into something else, which Paris has a history of since the collaborationist art of the Second World War. And so I developed an interest in art and language. There was a great poster in the Imperial War Museum, a French collaboration of a Nazi helmet in the sky with the SS insignia on the side, and underneath all these workers with their spanners in their overalls going towards their factories with zigzag roofs and big chimney stacks: 'Il donne sa sang, donnez votre travail' ['he gave his blood, give your work']. It's an incredible gag that's also pretty confrontational."

Such ideas further persuaded King that he should be an artist. "I wanted to be a fine artist, a painter. And it helped being in this incredibly intense little clique at school – it's only now that I realise how good it was." Bob White encouraged King to develop his interest in radical art, urging him to use the photo workshops to make 16mm films of experimental Sixties architecture and the so-called "cities in the sky". At 18, King was particularly fond of Marcel Duchamp, whom he found "the most wonderful thing in the world".

"It wasn't like most art departments, where they'd sit around wondering if they could do a copy of Monet's water lilies," says King. "The art that we were being encouraged to investigate was playful and challenging, intellectual and politically quite radical." He cites as an example "the bastard grandchildren of the Dadaists – I'm thinking of John Heartfield's satirical photo montages of Hitler in the Thirties such as *The Butter Is Finished*".

King's radical leanings were beginning to be expressed in political activism. He would later live "in and around Brixton", but wasn't involved in the Seventies or Eighties riots. But he felt an affinity with the rioting students of Paris '68. "The thing that characterised the Paris riots was it was students and workers together – not just getting angry with the cops. Generally, getting angry with the cops gets you get nowhere because the cops will win."

His empathy for dangerous scenarios was matched by a penchant for high-energy pop and incendiary rock'n'roll. "The music I most liked was Motown and the reggae stuff on Trojan. That was what Andy and I locked into. And we were obsessed with Jimi Hendrix and played *Axis: Bold As Love* and *Electric Ladyland* until the vinyl was rubbed into nothingness. There was nothing like listening to 'Voodoo Chile (Slight Return)': it's the most brilliant piece of existential music ever recorded.

"I also loved Roxy Music and David Bowie. He was brilliant, and his whole androgynous look really annoyed people. By the time I was 15/16 I'd become a huge fan of the Velvets, which was serendipitous because my friend's dad was a journalist for *The Sunday Times* and he got sent all these records, so I had an original copy of the *Velvet Underground & Nico* album with the removable sticker. Everybody knew about the Velvets, The MC5 and The Stooges – we all went up to London in 1972 to see The Stooges at the Scala cinema. They were fucking brilliant."

As much as the music, the experimental filmmakers of the period fascinated King. He even made a poster for Lindsay

Anderson's controversial 1968 movie *If…*, in which a group of schoolboys go on a killing spree, while he was at school.

"Film was a massive part of my life," he says. "I loved the whole existential approach: films like *The Goalkeeper's Fear Of The Penalty Kick* – the Sartrian or Camus-like idea that only by doing something can you fully realise yourself. So you're the goalkeeper and you've been predetermined to save the ball – it's immense bollocks now, but people took seriously the idea that you could actually take control of your life by not doing what you're most determined to do…

"I also liked the inventive language in *A Clockwork Orange*, all that fake Russian stuff. What the hooligans do in *A Clockwork Orange* is pointless. And, of course, one of the great things about rejecting your determination is not doing what's expected of you. Being pointless in itself is quite interesting but that was one of the big ideas of the situationists – being a 'flâneur' and doing silly things like walking slowly in a shopping precinct as a form of disruption."

King left Sevenoaks School in summer 1973, although he soon found himself back there. "I wanted to get my portfolio together and go to university," he says. "I wanted to do a foundation course, so Bob White arranged for me to stay on and teach at school. I taught art for three months, for a few hours a week, in exchange for all my materials. I was a teaching assistant at the age of 18. It was brilliant. I was teaching these 11-year-olds how to do Jackson Pollock paintings."

After his brief stint as a teacher, King experienced proletarian life first-hand when he got a job in a paper-sack factory for a few months in summer 1973. He was "a charge hand", and had to count the stitches on the paper sacks so they would come through in bundles of 50. He was, he says, "really good at that". They even offered him a full-time job – "I was quite chuffed."

He didn't accept the position; instead, he decided to use the money he'd earned to hitchhike round north-east America.

Unfortunately, the money didn't go very far due to gaps in his knowledge of US geography.

"I went to stay with a mate who was living in Buffalo, which, contrary to what I thought, was 450 miles away from New York City. So I flew into New York and thought I'd get a taxi there. But I didn't have very much money. And they said, 'No, no, you're an idiot – it's close to Toronto, near Niagara Falls!'"

The reason King wanted to go to Buffalo, he says, was to visit the Albright Knox Gallery, "which had a fantastic collection of art, and because there had been all these student riots there. I was wandering around with these yippies, who showed me their sniping positions, which was cool. I was only 18 and a bit of a loafer."

King then travelled up to New York where he "mooched around" for a week or so, staying in cheap motels because he'd run out of money and didn't want to ask his parents to bail him out – "not because they wouldn't have given it to me, but because they wouldn't have been able to afford it." He visited the Museum Of Modern Art before heading down to Washington DC and finally up to Philadelphia, "to see the Arensberg Collection and the Duchamp stuff."

King denies having any Bolshevik revolutionary tendencies at this point, although, "I knew who the enemy were – the ludicrously corrupt people who ran the country – and like any sensible person I'd read some Marx, but I wouldn't have called myself a Marxist. I was Labour in theory but I can't say I voted for the Labour Party – I would have thought of them as being dangerously right wing. I mean, Harold Wilson, what a ridiculous man. I was more interested in art and culture than politics. I found politics boring."

★   ★   ★

Dave Allen was born in December 1955 into a "simple working-class family", in Kendal, Cumbria, "the gateway to the Lakes", a small town of about 20,000 people and one record shop. He says he was the first in his family to develop an arty bent.

"I'm the one who got handed the creative gene – if you go back through my family history, it just didn't exist before me. Everyone got up, went to work and then, you know, died. Education wasn't part of it. It was like: 'You didn't get your A levels? Never mind, we've got a job here for you.'"

Allen's father was a do-anything type: "On my birth certificate it says, 'Father's job: journeyman', which is just another word for jack of all trades. He was an amazing painter and decorator. He could hang wallpaper, and you couldn't find the seam. He was insanely good. So it's actually not fair to say there wasn't a creative bone in anyone's body – he had it. So did my grandfather – you can see the lineage."

Allen has fond memories of his childhood and his parents' conventional roles, whereby his mother would "pack my dad's lunch box and flask and he'd go to work from eight to five, and when he came home he'd expect his meat and two veg on the table. It was all very simple."

His mother did have an occasional job, on the till at Marks & Spencer, but eventually she and Allen's father took over a fish and chip business "because he was sick of constantly doing painting and decorating", a move that Allen feels allowed them to move up the class ladder, albeit only slightly.

"We ended up buying a house, which was a big break because we lived on a council estate," he says. "Before I left home, they were morphing into middle-class, or lower-middle-class. They had a mortgage and a car and they were good parents. But they weren't pushing any of us towards college."

Allen was a fairly keen student at Kendal Grammar School, a boys' school with a girls' school attached, where he excelled at English and geography as well as chemistry and maths, although he was particularly fond of art. He gained "a few basic O levels" as well as A levels in English, geography and art. University, however, was never on the agenda.

"I could have gone, but it was never thought of as an option," he says. "I didn't have any friends who went – they just got jobs in town. You had your girlfriend in town – that was the centre of the earth. I'd never visited London – it was 250 miles away."

After leaving school, Allen left home to live in the centre of town and found a job in the printing department of the local branch of K Shoes, which he could have pursued as a vocation. Instead, in summer 1974 he decided to hitchhike to the south of France, to spend a month and a half grape-picking with three friends – including Nick Welsh, the son of a diplomat, and Welsh's brother Richard, who later, bizarrely, was assassinated in Greece by left wing forces.

"It was such fun," remembers Allen, who describes himself as "gregarious, a really sociable person – people just gravitate towards me." He continues: "We'd pick grapes to get pocket money and spend it on wine and bread. We were pushing 18: we weren't ready to become adults but were old enough to do things, even if we were responsible enough not to get into trouble. Not that we didn't do stupid things. I've got a great picture of me on the outskirts of Avignon, in the ruins of some ancient castle, standing up there with a drop of several hundred feet onto the rocks below, shirt off, with a bottle of wine in one hand – just doing the lad thing, you know? It was, like, one false step and there wouldn't have been any Gang Of Four."

Back in England, Allen decided to enrol in a graphic design course at Morecambe and Lancaster Tech, a community college, although he wasn't sure this was the direction he wanted to take. Then he heard that Nick Welsh had gone to Leeds University, so Allen "looked into continuing my education there – anything but working! So I moved to Leeds and buggered around for a bit, going to the campus with Nick. I was feeling a bit lost. That's when I saw the ad for a bassist and everything changed course."

★ ★ ★

Hugo Burnham was born on March 25, 1956, and grew up in Kent in a town called Cranbrook, attending Cranbrook School, not far from Gill and King's school in Sevenoaks. Not that he even met his future Gang-mates at this point.

"I was a bit of a sports nut at the time, so I went over to Sevenoaks School to play rugby, but I never ran into them."

The eldest of five children, Burnham's family was, he says, "essentially middle-class. My dad was in the rag trade in London, in the fashion business, and we went to prep school and then grammar school." There, he was in the school orchestra, evincing a penchant for drumming early on.

"I wanted a drum kit for years, because I used to play the snare drum in my prep school orchestra," he says, "and I kept trying to get a drum kit. Eventually I started going up to London on my own or with my dad, hanging around Charing Cross Road and all the music stores and bash out a terrible attempt at 'Stairway To Heaven'. One time I saw this Olympic drum kit and convinced my dad to let me use my savings to buy it – that was my first kit."

Burnham played in the school band for a year and a half before getting sidetracked by A levels. He had no inclination to go to university – he tried to get into the Central School Of Drama but failed – and so he spent the first year after school "just bumming around, not really getting anywhere". He came "within a hair's breadth" of joining the Royal Navy.

"I didn't know what to do, and the Navy seemed like a bit of a laugh," he admits. "I could travel and, because I was a bit of a sports nut, I thought I could play rugby there, that sort of thing. So I took all the interviews and tests. They got down to the last few applicants, and I was supposed to get on a train to go down to Southampton for the weekend, but it coincided with getting tickets to see a band with my brother at the Palladium. So I sent the train ticket back to the Navy and said, 'I don't think this is a good idea after all.'"

He spent the summer doing odd jobs, working for the local

pottery, where his younger brother Jol worked. After a while, he thought, "Christ, I've got to get out of here", so he applied for a university place through the "clearing" system, and purely by chance wound up at Leeds, where he would study English and theatre.

CHAPTER 2

THE HISTORY OF THE WHIRL

"What were Gang Of Four about? Each member of the band will give you different answers. It could be as simple as, 'We were the most groundbreaking post-punk band to come out of Britain in 1978.' Or, 'We were the most lyrically intelligent band to ever put a record out and not be too pompous.' Or, 'The band who played a part in helping women break through in rock music.' We would do anything to improve women's rights, just as we would go on Rock Against Racism tours. Gang Of Four were about politics with a small 'p' – the stuff that affects your daily life. Not party politics. Although I do like to party."
– Dave Allen

A ndy Gill, Jon King, Dave Allen and Hugo Burnham all arrived in Leeds just before punk broke. But already the university had become a hotbed of radical activity and provocative thinking, much of which fed into the music and lyrics that the quartet would write for Gang Of Four.

Leeds University's fine art department spawned Gang Of Four, The Mekons and Delta 5, encouraging a conceptual approach where theory meets artistic practice. Tim Clark, the department head, was a member of the British chapter of the Situationist International. Terry Atkinson, the studio-painting tutor, once belonged to Art & Language, who drew on Marxism and hard-core aesthetic theory. This all helped fuel GOF's sarcastic, combative approach, their meta-rock, which was radically self-analytical and vigilant.

It was a time of change: late 1975 when, according to Burnham, "suddenly, big, white, flared trousers were disappearing." Still very much the sports nut, Gang Of Four's future drummer immediately joined the Rugby Club, although not for long. "It lasted about six weeks," he recalls, "until I realised what an absolute bunch of tossers they all were. Their idea of fun was standing on a table with their trousers round their ankles, drinking and singing. I was like, 'This isn't for me.' And I was doing a lot of acting and theatre stuff as well, and the rugby crowd didn't like that. I was a fucking southern fairy."

A southern fairy with a close crop, dressed in Doc Martens and drainpipe jeans – Burnham looked every inch the proto-punk rocker, a good six months before punk broke. Soon the English undergraduate joined an experimental theatre company (although they weren't, as has previously been reported, informed by the writings of Karl Marx). He remembers spying his future bandmates, Andy Gill and Jon King, for the first time across a crowded student union bar – they were "the freaks with the short hair and the straight trousers", notably Gill, who used to stride around the university campus in a long, brown leather coat that Burnham craved.

"He looked so cool, so I introduced myself," he says. "I started hanging out with him and Jon a little bit. They were part of the fine art crowd. I kept seeing them at the same places – reggae dances and at the bar. I slowly got involved with them on a social level."

In a frictional relationship with the fine art crowd were the anarchist crew, and there was, according to Burnham, "definite animosity between the two groups", although instead of ideological debates or fist-fights their disagreements took the form of "scowling and growling." The fist-fights came when the National Front started appearing in Leeds, and then the animosity disappeared and the two camps became one oppositional force.

Agrees Gill: "There was fairly constant strife between National Front representatives and people on the left, which on many occasions broke out into street violence or violence in pubs. Sometimes, people from the NF would attempt to do marches through the middle of town, people would come out to demonstrate and then the police would come out."

Jon King had originally intended to go to Newcastle University because of his admiration for Richard Hamilton, the Duchamp expert, a lecturer there. But he eventually settled on Leeds where another hero, Lawrence Gowring, a world expert on Cezanne and Vermeer, lectured. He remembers his interview well.

"He had this tremendous speech impediment – he'd had a quite serious illness – and he said, 'Y-y-you must be J-J-Jonathan', and this great lump of flob shot out of his mouth onto his tie. He just wiped it away and said, 'Would you like a sherry?' I thought he was great. His lectures were electrifying and, if you didn't turn up early, you didn't get a seat."

As Gang Of Four's principal lyricist, King's project was, broadly speaking, to question everything and regard much of everyday reality as an illusion. His penchant was for art with dual meanings. "I had a Vichy French franc coin from 1942 that said, instead of 'liberte, egalite, fraternite' [liberty, equality, friendship], 'famille, travail, patrie' [work, family, country]. I thought it was incredibly interesting that you could have the core idea of the battle between progressiveness and reaction on this coin: work, family and country against friendship, equality and freedom. It was amazing that this collaborationist government could be so crystallised on a coin, so that every day people were reminded they were part of a reactionary environment."

This sort of subversive art would become Gang Of Four's forte – in fact, the Vichy coin provided the front cover image of the band's 1990 compilation, *A Brief History Of The Twentieth Century*. King tapped into the rising, seething discontent that he detected in Britain at the time of his arrival at Leeds. Like Gill, he remembers aggro between left and right spilling out onto the streets of Leeds.

"The country was seen to be almost ungovernable," he recalls. "Something had to be done. In 1975, Andy and I went to a British Movement demonstration – they wanted to march through the centre of Leeds with all their flags. It was quite outrageous, so they were banned by Leeds Council. But they held a private meeting inside a public building. So I joined a modest-sized demonstration outside and had a very pleasant day chatting to the cops, keeping quiet till the British Movement decided they were going to walk down to the railway station, which was effectively doing what they had been banned from doing.

"As soon as they came out, the cops completely lost control of everything and immediately started attacking the demonstrators. I was truncheoned down by a mounted cop. Andy was practically crushed against a wall. You saw how the uniforms reacted to an assault on democracy and equality to defend work, family and country. It was instantaneous."

Not that King threw in his lot with the Revolutionary Communist Party or any other of the student rebel factions on offer at Leeds University. "I didn't like the sound of them. They were all interested in politics, and I wasn't. Actually, the best-looking girls were in the Socialist Workers Party. And the most interesting women were Trotskyists. But I'm not a Trotskyist. And the Communists were still trying to justify Stalin and all of that terrible business."

Gill remembers Leeds being very bleak during this period, especially if you didn't have much money. It was, he recalls, "a boring, student kind of existence. It wasn't a very comfortable place to be." It was literally uncomfortable for Gill, who spent a couple of months living in university halls of residence before moving into a basement flat in Hyde Park, off St John's Terrace.

"It was permanently wet," he remembers. "It was disgusting. I was sharing a little bedroom, a kitchen and a living room with another student. The halls were warm and dry, but I chose the damp and cold. You had to keep a fire going all the time: I'd find council fencing and fallen branches, and had to keep getting paraffin. They were squalid conditions, and I had a cold for nine months of the year, from September to April."

At one point, he even ended up "living in a communal situation" with members of The Mekons, although it wasn't quite as hippie-trippy as that sounds. "I was never keen on dope," he insists. "I think I did a bit of speed every now and then, and mushrooms. Nobody was particularly druggy. We'd go down the boozer a bit…"

In fact, King and Gill were, even prior to punk, fighting a rearguard action against the remains of the Class of '67. "We all had really short hair, and leather jackets and stuff," says King. "I'd been a lifelong motorcyclist and had a Ducati 1000, while Andy had a Honda 250 that he once fit 12 or 13 people on! But our look had nothing to do with punk, because punk didn't yet exist. It was pure function, not posture. Well, a bit of posture, but more to piss off middle-class students than to look like a greaser."

Either way, King and Gill really stood out in Leeds, especially when they went to discos and interrupted the DJs' usual 'Hi Ho Silver Lining' to ask for 'Double Barrel' by Dave & Ansel Collins. Still, as he puts it, "The more renegade women would be like, 'Thank God there's a trouble-making young man here!'" Unfortunately, these trouble-makers made a less positive impression on Leeds' young males, rubbing up the townies the wrong way. "There was a big problem between the university and the locals – a lot of it was around extreme right-wing politics," says King. "Sometimes they would come up to the university and beat up students – we were OK because we were down the town the whole time, and we probably looked less like students than some of the other ones; we didn't have the accoutrements of studentdom."

Unusually for a fine art undergraduate, King also had an air gun. He used to share a flat with Andy Corrigan and Mark White of The Mekons; they had an air pistol with which they would try to shoot mice, although mainly they would miss. Corrigan, a particularly bad shot, would shoot all the plates out in the kitchen instead.

★ ★ ★

Throughout 1976, alongside an atmosphere of right vs left unrest in Leeds were other punk-fuelled feelings. These included the notions proposed by, respectively, Richard Hell & The Voidoids and The Sex Pistols of a 'Blank Generation' and of being 'Pretty Vacant'. Some took these to signify opportunities for self-reinvention, others as nihilistic rejections of everything.

"Nihilism was the idea that everything was fucked-up so nothing matters – destroy or whatever," says King, who wasn't completely convinced. "They were funny, almost cartoonish ideas, but I'm not sure how interesting they were. The Sex Pistols' *Never Mind The Bollocks* just sounded like speeded-up Black Sabbath with funny lyrics to me, although not as funny as the lyrics by The Ramones, which were genuinely comic and hilarious."

At this point, King maintains that he wasn't any more interested in being a musician than he was when he was at school. He felt more disposed towards the idea of forming a band, however, following a trip he and Gill made to New York in September 1976: King got a research grant to study Jasper Johns in New York, while Gill "blagged a grant" to do a photographic study of Gothic architecture, enabling him to buy a ticket as well. The pair stayed with a "friend of a friend" called Mary Harron, then a rock writer for New York's *Punk* magazine and later the director of *American Psycho*.

"We stayed with her in her shit little apartment in a brownstone in Greenwich Village on St Marks Place, which is about four blocks from CBGBs," recalls King. "She'd been going out with Patti Smith's drummer, JD Daugherty, so she knew everybody. We'd go down every night to CBGBs, where The Ramones and Richard Hell & The Voidoids would hang out. They assumed we were in a band because we were British – at that stage, everybody thought British people were interesting. I found the New York bands interesting – they were all very arty, into Rimbaud and stuff. I loved Television – that spiky, meandering guitar stuff, and Tom Verlaine's way of singing like someone had put a carrot up his arse."

By the time they returned from their pilgrimage to New York, punk had began to make an impact on Leeds. Andy Corrigan was even photographed on the front cover of the Leeds-published *Yorkshire Evening Post* wearing a penis earring. For Gill, who hadn't had long hair since he was 14, punk didn't evince a radical shift in musical direction; rather it was "a very slow development going back to the beginning of the Seventies", an extension of the sort of furious R&B purveyed by Dr Feelgood.

By this time, Gill and King had written a few "silly songs" on an acoustic guitar and an old cassette player under the influence of Dr Feelgood, a band they had seen live a dozen times. "We used to write comic songs, a bit dumb – they were R&B in the old sense: verse, chorus, bridge, chorus, outro, that kind of thing." One song stood out because it was rather less conventional and rooted in tradition: 'Anthrax', later a prime example of Gang Of Four's radical approach to songcraft, which they sketched out on a piece of paper, musically as well as lyrically. "Jon and I would work on these ideas like a scientific formula – 'repetitive drum beat here, feedback guitar noise here'," says Gill. "We'd sit and play guitar for days on end, start a game of chess, drink gin and strum a bit, then write a song. 'I Found That Essence Rare' was another one."

Around this time there were two signal musical events, and you can imagine the nascent Gang making connections between them in the air: Dr Feelgood's *Stupidity* reached number one, and Bob

Marley & The Wailers appeared at a now legendary gig at London's Lyceum, which Gill and King attended. "We were into ska when we were 16 but, by the time we were 19, we were hearing proper reggae," says Gill. "I really liked I Roy, who was halfway between ska and dub. There were people who really liked reggae and saw it as some powerful force to be reckoned with, while others thought Desmond Decker was quite funny but that generally it was stupid."

They were working in a vacuum at the time: "Leeds didn't have any kind of scene at all," he recalls. "After a while we came up with a few ideas we thought were quite interesting." But soon, the idea occurred that they should form a band.

First, they needed a name. One day early in 1977, Corrigan, Gill and King were driving through Leeds when they saw a newspaper billboard that read: "Gang Of Four On Trial", a reference to the deposed leftist faction led by Chairman Mao's widow who attempted to seize power in Communist China after his death. Corrigan thought it would make a great name for a band, and so Gang Of Four it was. The name had nothing to do with the "big four" structuralist theorists – Claude Lévi-Strauss, Michel Foucault, Roland Barthes and Jacques Lacan – as some have suggested, possibly the result of the band getting bored with answering the same questions in interviews and either making facts up or telling barefaced lies to amuse themselves. Immediately, the band acquired a reputation for being "neo-Marxist rock'n'rollers".

"Taking that name was a serious joke," reflects Gill. "The idea of four British scruffs naming themselves after these important Maoist cultural revolutionaries: it was ridiculous. But that's what appealed about it, making a ridiculous claim for our importance at a time when we were totally unimportant. Because it was also saying, 'We WILL be cultural revolutionaries.'"

"It was meant as a joke but immediately we were 'commie band Gang Of Four,'" laughs Allen. "To this day we're seen as raging lunatic Maoists, commie bastards or, at best, socialists." This impression was intensified by the band's habit of approaching virtually everything they did with a sort of missionary zeal, whether it was helping set up Rock Against Racism or drunkenly planning an eight-hour mission to Margate to buy "proper" fish and chips. "We were obsessive," remembers King. They attracted lazy headlines about "dour, northern commies", but few realised the humour behind stunts like posing as Chinese cultural revolutionaries on the steps of Leeds town hall.

The first recruit to King and Gill's new venture was Hugo Burnham, with whom the pair had begun to hang around. "I saw Jon and Andy play with a guy I played rugby with called Speedy on drums," recalls Burnham. "He wasn't terribly good. They just sort of jammed. And then a couple of months later it was like, 'Well, I've got a drum kit,' and I actually hadn't, but I did a week later because I went and got one for fifty quid. And we had our first rehearsal in Andrew's basement flat, playing through a couple of songs. And one of the people there I remember was Mick Wicksy, who ended up being The Mekons' first manager. He had long black hair, a real greaser, with a filthy leather jacket – he'd been part of a quite serious bike gang in the north. Lovely guy, though. And he either said, 'That's fucking great' or 'That's fucking awful' about me, I can't remember."

According to King, Burnham had uses beyond an ability to play the drums. "Hugo used to nick stuff. He'd go into a music shop with one of those big A1 artist's portfolios, and he'd hide a cymbal inside it," he marvels.

The band's original bassist was Dave Wolfson, also known as Wolfman, "a real hippie kind of guy, a very nice bloke but really a space cadet", according to Dave Allen. "He used to sit cross-legged and wanted to jam all the time. Still, he played bass for two shows, and then we all broke off for the summer."

The four-piece couldn't find anywhere to play live. The main places to hang out in Leeds at the time were Terry's All Night Cafe, which specialised in chip butties, and the Heaven And Hell Club, which specialised in lager and violence. There was also the International Club in Chapeltown, which played decent black music. A bloke called John Keenan used to put on gigs like the 'F' Club, which moved around different venues, and there was one band called SOS doing punk stuff, but that was about it before the line-up of Gill, King, Burnham and Wolfson played their first gig in April 1977 in the basement of Leeds' Corn Exchange – one of the very first alternative shows in Leeds.

"It was pretty intense and full-on – very enjoyable almost immediately. After two or three shows, however, we realised that Dave Wolfson was not the right guy to play bass because, although a really good musician, he approached it in a kind of jazz-funk workout kind of way," says Gill. "Put it this way: it didn't sound like dub reggae."

That first gig was a memorable night, not least because the concert was stormed by local National Front bootboys – Leeds was a stronghold of the NF and the British Movement. Remembers Burnham: "In those days you never knew quite where anyone stood. If it was punk then it was just as likely to be right as it was left – and there was a bit of confusion because of my short hair, but skinheads came looking for a fight. So Andy swung a guitar at someone's face and I think a couple of bottles went flying."

Gill remembers there being a spiky atmosphere, but denies smashing his guitar over a skinhead's head – "there was no contact between head and guitar, skinhead or otherwise," he insists. He does agree, however, that Gang Of Four, particularly he and King, were at this point "quite bolshy characters", while their gigs had become sites for pitched battles. "There was this constant thing with the NF and BNP where they'd come looking for 'lefty' students, and there'd be glasses and tables flying everywhere," he says. Sometimes the violence was so extreme it made him re-consider the combative nature of GOF's music.

On the whole, though, it was, says Burnham, a successful first foray: "It was quite good fun. One of the first songs was called 'Gang

Of Four' and it went, 'We're the Gang Of Four!' and Dave would be spouting Chinese gibberish. It was arty but not arty-farty."

"It was fairly frantic stuff," adds Gill. "'Return The Gift' was in that first set. We already had a lot of ideas. Punk had arrived and I loved the Pistols and The Clash, although I thought the Pistols were just speeded-up heavy metal with growly stuff on top. I'm not sure if we had the same agenda as them."

The band's next gig came a month later in the Tartan Bar of the student union, downstairs at the back, in a line-up comprising three bands: headliners Severed Head & The Neckfuckers, with Gill doing sound and Burnham in charge of lights; Gang Of Four themselves; and the opening band – the very first incarnation of The Mekons, who came on in a "spaceship", in reality an old sofa.

"Two of them pushed the other one on – Mark White and Andy Corrigan, the two singers," says Burnham. "They did three songs, including 'Fight The Cops'. It was hilarious."

As for Gang Of Four, Burnham remembers the set: "We played 'Elevator' – 'Waiting for my elevator/I'm thinking I should have come later' – that track 'Gang Of Four', a song called 'John Stonehouse' – 'John Stonehouse went for a swim, John Stonehouse got to jack it in' – and an early version of 'Damaged Goods', which was originally called 'Love Not Lust'. And we played the end of 'Day Tripper' by The Beatles."

It was after the band's first couple of live forays that they realised they needed some decent equipment to match their fast-evolving sound, so they decided to build their own PA system. With the resourceful Andy Corrigan something of a handyman, he worked out how to make a PA from speakers once used to broadcast propaganda from bomber aircraft, which they found in an army surplus store. Unfortunately, at an early GOF gig at Nottingham's Rock City, they had a bit of a Spinal Tap moment when they tried to get Corrigan's home-made speakers through the doors but they were so big.

At this point, the band were influenced by Free, Jimi Hendrix,

Funkadelic and Dr. Feelgood: a right rhythmic racket. Their pioneering sound was stumbled on as Gill attempted reggae and came up with a unique, feedback-ridden noise once described as "pigeons crashing through a grand piano". Gradually, they developed a manifesto: "No corny lyrics, no obvious melodies and no change of key." They weren't just "not corny"; their lyrics had intellectual rigour. "The personal is political, everything is political" were phrases that abounded in the music press of the time, and there were heated debates about internal affairs and external issues in most radically minded bands back then. Gang Of Four were more rigorous than most.

"'Rigorous' is a word other people use about us more than ourselves, although I think we were rigorous in that what we didn't want to do was be fucking obvious," considers Burnham. "Our agenda was like, 'OK, we're not going to sing about this, so we've got to write about this.' Jon obviously was the prime mover, lyrically. Andy would probably say, 'Hey, what about me, too?' I had nothing to do with lyrics at all, other than 'It's Her Factory', which came later – I sang it. It started off as a real punky-reggae dark jam. It came from a story in *The Sun* about women being closer to the earth, more natural, all that bollocks. So I said, 'Yeah, closer to the earth, scrubbing the floor.'"

Not that they sat around all day discussing what was and wasn't "ideologically sound" or "right on" – the late Seventies equivalents of "politically correct". "It wasn't as dour and serious as that," says Burnham. "We'd talk about it while we were drunk or in the pub. It was a conversation we'd have a) being essentially art students, and b) being not fucking dickheads. We were more politically aware than politically active."

Situated exactly between the university and the polytechnic, the site for many of these heated debates was a pub called The Fenton, where early rehearsals took place upstairs. It was the boozer of choice for Leeds' blossoming punk fraternity and a frequent target for National Front bootboys, who would terrorise punters by smashing in windows and the occasional student skull. The members of Gang Of Four and The Mekons, as well as other Leeds luminaries such as Delta 5, Marc Almond and Green Gartside of Scritti Politti, would colonise the little room at the back of the pub and drink and argue long into the night, the new breed of radicals and nonconformists in their leather coats and Doc Martens.

"We were very territorial about it," says Burnham. "We'd sit there, all of us in this little room staring at each other, drunk, trying to provoke each other into things. There were arguments about what was good or bad – we didn't talk about music very much."

King made sure things didn't get too worthier-than-thou. "I couldn't stand those people because I didn't think they had any fun," he says. "They never seemed to get laid, get in fights or upset anybody. I thought that seemed incredibly tedious."

Allen has vivid memories of the firebrand atmosphere. "We had very little money – we'd not eat so we could go to the pub. And it was the epicentre. I was moderating a panel in Seattle recently about social networking and I got them all laughing immediately about how, when I was growing up with Gang Of Four, that was called 'going to the pub'. Anything you needed to know was down the pub. All the gossip, all the news, all the 'who's doing what to who and who's having sex with who, and do you realise who got drunk last night and had sex with that guy's girlfriend and, wow that's a problem?' It was really funny in a British sitcom way. But we had a blast there. We got friggin' pissed every night. We loved it. There was a real mixture of thinkers and drinkers, and everyone had opinions."

*   *   *

All Gang Of Four needed now was a decent bassist. An ad posted on the wall of the student union in summer 1977, written in Feelgood terms, read: "Fast rivvum & blues band requires a fast rivvum & blues bass player." To Allen, that spelling of rhythm was like a code, "so I knew I was on the right track". Allen, who'd had stints as a session bassist and a truck driver and was then hanging round Leeds looking for direction, responded immediately.

"I answered the ad, and did the audition, as did Mick Wicksy, who was a cool guy but he couldn't really play the bass that well. I was the only real candidate; we got together and did our thing and the rest is history. I always played the bass. When I was in my teens I messed around with an acoustic guitar, stuck a pick on it and imagined myself to be Jimi Hendrix. I couldn't quite get a handle on it but I've got quite a bit of rhythm. I can play drums a bit as well: I really enjoyed messing about and doing weird things with drum machines."

Allen, the working-class boy from the north, denies that he brought a "militant tendency" to the table or had any particular axe to grind. "All I knew was growing up in Kendal, and if you didn't vote Labour you were run out of town," he says. "It was very working class. And I understood enough of the class system. I noticed this growing up with my dad – if he had to work on a Saturday because he had to get a job finished, he'd ask me to come along and help him. We'd go to these opulent places and I saw how he acted in front of the upper crust, because the Lake District's full of money – old money for people with servants. And he was really subservient to them, which I hated. He'd do the old 'yes sir, no sir'. I'd go back to my bedroom and think about it all."

To Allen, Gill and King were from a different world, even if the differences between them weren't quite as vast as some have implied. "I knew they'd had life a bit better, but not that much better. There wasn't a huge class difference. We were all the same sort. I would always argue that I missed out on the education. Both Andy and Jon, their parents were at best lower middle-class but, because they were talented students, they got a fast track in a better school system and that really benefited them – that was the difference. Otherwise, we were all the same. Jon's family definitely struggled."

Nor does Jon King believe that Allen would have felt insecure being among three middle-class boys, or that he'd have felt intimidated by Gill and King's tendency towards intellectual bully-boy tactics. "I did have a fanatical pursuit of ideas but I don't know if that's good or bad," says King, "but that characterises me. I don't think we were very nice to be around, really. It was all endless fucking point scoring, or going off on flights of lunatic, extremist ideas.

"But I don't think with Dave it could possibly have been a class thing, because he and I were from exactly the same background. He went to a grammar school and I happened to go to a Direct Grant place, but his parents ran a fish and chip shop and my dad was an electrician. Classwise, I would have argued that I was more working class than him. I would have told him he was petty bourgeois. His parents owned a fucking shop! Fucking fascists! I say that in jest, but that would have been the extrapolation. A lot of it was probably just a north-south thing."

"There was nothing between those three and me," insists Allen. "If anything it was the media who tried to single me out as the working-class one. After a while it bothered me, like it was some badge of honour."

When Allen answered the advert, Gill and King were actually still on their sojourn in the States, checking out The Ramones et al, so the only member of the band that Allen met was Burnham. The drummer came to the door in a multi-coloured knitted sweater and ripped T-shirt, and had dyed blond hair and an earring. Equally striking was the skinhead bootboy's posh accent. "He was a funny figure," laughs Allen. "He talked so well. I didn't know what I'd walked into – I thought they were meant to be a punk band. Hugo was brought up in Kent and I think he had a pretty good living; he spoke almost Queen's English. He has some weird affectations, like calling people 'My good man'. I never confronted Hugo about that stuff. 'My good man' – it suggested a certain superiority. I'm not saying it's insensitive, but coming from a guy who's not an English toff but wants to be – that always puzzled me with Hugo. He'd say the weirdest things to people."

On Gill and King's return to England, charged up after seeing the more progressive, experimental CBGBs bands such as Television and Talking Heads – who were going way beyond the three-chord garage-land punk remit of their UK counterparts – the band took shape, and fast. "I fit in very quickly with the guys personally and musically," says Allen. "Andy and Jon suddenly realised that we did have something. I was just the catalyst that helped them become more formed."

Burnham describes Allen as "the outsider" when he first joined, but Burnham, Gill and King immediately recognised Allen's worth. "He was a real musician," marvels Burnham. "He had a great musical range, having played in brunch jazz, rock and pop bands for years. He came in with quite a canon of stuff."

King credits Allen's arrival as the catalyst for their rapid transformation into a serious performing unit. Almost immediately, he pushed the group into the punk-funk zone. An accomplished player, Allen wanted to make music "like Stevie Wonder but heavy". Gill and King, conversely, trained him to play more sparsely: "a quarter of the number of notes he was capable of playing."

"Dave was a grammar school boy and extremely bright – very similar to me, really," says King. "When he joined, everything changed. He was a really interesting musician, incredibly bright and talented. And he really knew how to have fun. Plus, he always liked funk – Dave could actually play that stuff. A song like 'Anthrax' could be played by almost anybody – it was a simple pattern. But 'Damaged Goods' or 'What We All Want' needed someone who could actually play. Reggae, Big Youth, Parliament-Funkadelic – he could do all that. But he wasn't too musicianly. It was more about ideas."

Allen, you could just tell, was a fan of Weather Report, Miles Davis, Bootsy Collins and the finger-popping style of Chic's

Bernard Edwards, as well as "the amazing funky music" of Gang Of Four's Bristolian contemporaries and counterparts, The Pop Group. He acknowledges his impact on the band, and the way his musical approach dovetailed nicely with Gill's rhythmical guitar playing, influenced by Wilko Johnson at his most funkily serrated. "I wasn't a strumming bass player doing one note – der der der di di der der der," he says. "I was funky."

Band rehearsals ensued in a room Gang Of Four shared with The Mekons in a run-down area of Leeds. Burnham and Allen, directed by Gill and King, would kick around ideas until half an hour before pub closing time. "Andy would play the drums and get things going, because he always thought rhythmically as well as melodically," says Allen, who remembers that Burnham was less than ecstatic at being instructed in how to play beats by the guitarist.

"He wasn't happy, but then, there's no argument that all of the drum parts are Andy's. Even if Hugo came up with a drum riff, Andy would jump in and go, 'Try it like this.' Hugo argued back – he can be very argumentative – but he realised pretty quickly that there was no point because it would deteriorate into he and Andy being at each other like dogs. It was insane."

The high-energy nature of the band's performances, the way they careened and slammed into each other on stage, was the natural corollary of the intensity of the music they were making. Gill recalls "running battles" – some of them humorous, others less so – during rehearsals over everything from lyrical content to the use of hi-hats. Mostly, these spats were between the guitarist and drummer. "Hugo threw his drumsticks at me quite a lot," says Gill. "It wasn't pleasant if it went in your eye. A lot of it was strongly held views about what we were doing. How it should be, how it should go. What we were trying to do. For the most part me and Jon agreed, but not me and Hugo…"

According to Allen, Burnham's dark moods were apparent early on. "Hugo has always been argumentative – he brings with him this sort of darkness. It was palpable: if he was in a certain mood he brought it to the rehearsal room." And yet, says Allen, despite Gill and King being the main ideas men, Gang Of Four was a democracy of sorts, with the various power plays between the four musicians providing the necessary tension to create such a dynamic racket.

"The input came from all angles," he says. "We were four people pulling and pushing and tugging, and that's what made it what it was. It wasn't about sitting down and working things out."

From the off, Gang Of Four's music was stark and severe: Gill shunned sound-thickening effects like fuzz and distortion, while Burnham eschewed splashy cymbals – "what I got from Andy was the less-is-more ethos. Don't fill the gaps. And I think we all realised that, yeah, this is much more exciting. Don't play normal four-on-the-floor beats, splash your cymbals or do rolls around the kit, because that's what everyone does." So the rule was: no solos; instead, anti-solos, where members stopped playing and left a hole. No valve amps, either, because they were too warm; instead, they used transistorised amps – for a more brittle, cleaner, colder sound. Gang Of Four were against warmth.

Nor were they into rock spontaneity. There would be no intuitive looseness, letting songs emerge organically out of jams. Everything was thought out in advance. Burnham, with Gill, devised mechanistic drum loops. All the instruments had their own space in the mix: guitar, bass and drums were on equal footing, the democratic sonic set-up reflecting the band's egalatarian ideals.

Gill's guitar shapes owed much to the furious, scratchy style of Dr Feelgood's Wilko Johnson. He and King also adored reggae and the cosmic funk of George Clinton: they'd later bemuse a new wave audience at York University by dancing on stage in a conga line with Factory Records boss Tony Wilson to the strains of Funkadelic's 'One Nation Under A Groove'. Equally anti-punk were the secret role models of Burnham (Free's Simon Kirke,

Charlie Watts of The Rolling Stones) and Allen (Weather Report/ Joni Mitchell bassist Jaco Pastorius). "If I'd have said that at the time," admits Allen, "I'd have been called a wanker."

The disparate approaches of the four musicians resulted in a violently danceable cacophony that was organic and original. They scrutinised every last note with merciless precision. "The idea was to unpick new music, whether it was disco or funk, and put it back together in an original form," says Gill, "to consider every last drum beat. There was constant discussion."

Gang Of Four thrived on friction, with Gill the master of the put-down. Prickly, like his guitar playing, he was influenced by Wilko's jagged, choppy rhythm-as-lead style. They all loved not just Dr Feelgood's stripped-down sound but the aura of barely contained violence.

"We argued all the time about everything," maintains King. "It was a continuous assault on each other, a constant state of having a go. Even on stage, it was like an orchestrated fight between us. But the real thing that powered the band was probably drinking."

But how good were the Gang Of Four members on their respective instruments? Dave Allen considers them to have been up there with the best of the post-punk scene and beyond. "I considered myself a really good bass player," he says. "And Andy was tremendous; his talent was extraordinary. He was the best rhythm guitarist of his generation, for the whole post-punk scene. The way he played guitar, the structure of the riffs… Hugo was very good for Gang Of Four, even though I'm not sure how far his skills would have taken him – if Led Zeppelin phoned up, I don't know if he could do that. But there's never been another band like Gang Of Four. Everyone's taken pieces of it and used it to their own benefit, but there's never been a band like us."

CHAPTER 3

THAT ESSENCE RARE

"Out of confrontation and challenge comes great noise. We cared about what we were doing so we would argue, absolutely – whether it was about the music, the performance or the price of a bloody Mars bar. I was always more in conflict with Andy, but I had the greatest time of my life as a young man with those three guys. We were committed. God, we were committed." – Hugo Burnham

Twenty months passed between Gang Of Four's first gig and their debut single, 'Damaged Goods', and, although this period in the band's development is barely documented, that doesn't mean they weren't busy. In fact, they were gigging fairly relentlessly, honing the fury of their live sound in preparation for their first recorded assault and accruing a big following on the student circuit. One of the benefits of having Dave Allen, a non-student, in their ranks was that he was able to devote time and energy to getting the band plenty of live work.

"Our ascent was really quick, and one of the reasons we got gigs was by my not enrolling in college," he says. "Prior to my arrival there wasn't a lot of organisation, and it wasn't that I brought organisation, it was just that when I turned up I was perhaps the missing piece that caused the thing to gel. And I had the time to get to a payphone and bug people about the band. I actually came down to London once with the useless endeavour of wandering about town and meeting people. We wanted a booking agent; we weren't really looking for a record deal. I wasn't managing the band, that's way too much of a stretch, but I was making the phone calls. And it was from one of those phone calls that we heard about the Buzzcocks playing at Ilkley College, about 20 miles from Leeds."

It was November 1977, and Manchester's Buzzcocks were arguably the biggest punk band outside of London, so Allen harassed Ilkley College's student union five times a day for two weeks, a series of phone calls during which the bassist would sing his band's praises, only to be met with bemused replies of "Gang of what?" Eventually, he wrote a letter to the union booking agent, saying they'd be a perfect match for the Buzzcocks, and they won the support slot. "He relented," says Allen, "or I beat him down. So God bless him. It was no money, £30 or something, but we didn't care; we just wanted to get in front of a national band's audience and play."

After the show, the Buzzcocks' manager, Richard Boon, was sufficiently impressed to ask for the band's details. "He sort of fell in love with us," says Hugo Burnham. Shortly afterwards, a telegram arrived at Allen's home in Leeds, inviting Gang Of Four to support the Buzzcocks on tour to promote the latter's March 1978 debut album, *Another Music In A Different Kitchen*. "I'd never had a telegram before," recalls Allen, "and it was like, 'Who's died? What's wrong with my parents?'" It was from Richard Boon, and it read: "Buzzcocks tour of Europe and UK – stop – Want Gang Of Four – stop – Call immediately – stop."

The Ilkley gig was, says Allen, "the one where I proved my chops on stage and was finally totally accepted." The tour also exposed Gang Of Four to a wider audience, including many rock journalists, and earned them their first live date in the capital at The National in Kilburn. This was a must-see show for which there were queues around the block – more for Gang Of Four than for the headliners, The Soft Boys, Robyn Hitchcock's band, who had a monthly residency there. "We felt sorry for them, because nobody came to see them that night," he says. "But it was a breakthrough for us. It was perfect. We were used to playing in Leeds, in small rooms and on cramped stages, with everyone packed together. We were ready for something bigger."

After the Ikley and National shows came a spate of high-profile support slots with The Slits and Siouxsie & The Banshees – in fact, GOF were there when the Banshees' original drummer, Kenny Morris, and guitarist, John McKay, "took a powder" and disappeared. Although Gang Of Four would soon acquire a reputation for being dour intellectuals – postgraduated heavy-metal funk; Hendrix meets Marx – who'd decided that modern life was, if not rubbish, then certainly ripe for dissection, as well as for attacking rock'n'roll convention, during this period they were a bunch of young musicians on the road, having fun.

"We had a blast," says Burnham. "There was always that thing of, 'Oh, they're just a fucking support act, fuck 'em.' But we managed to get along well with all the road crews, who used to give us everything we wanted. We were always proud that we weren't assholes. We might have been known later on as intellectuals, but we were hard-drinking, hard-living intellectuals who had, you know, fun.

"We were 21, 22, and we were in a rock band on the road," he continues. "Were we disrespectful to women? No. Were we monastic? No. We weren't puritanical. We were well-spoken, but we were interesting. We just didn't talk bollocks. We were politically aware, and somewhat politically active. But if a journalist was with us it wasn't like, 'Oh, let's pretend we're monastic do-gooders.' We might have had collectivist ideals, sharing equipment and rehearsal space with The Mekons and Delta 5 and paying everyone the same money, including the roadies, we might have had principles, but we knew how to make a big, bloody, rhythmic racket, and we knew how to enjoy ourselves."

Allen concurs: "We resisted the rock'n'roll lifestyle as much as we could, but we were a party band. We were pretty heavy-drinking. Whatever went with that went with that. It wasn't stupid bacchanalia. We weren't Led Zeppelin, but we weren't morose, boring and depressed about the state of the world. We had a real good time, although if we ran into women backstage, ironically we'd end up having conversations with them."

Influenced by Free, musically if not lyrically, Gang Of Four were, according to Simon Reynolds' post-punk history, *Rip It Up And Start Again*, "cock-rock castrated". In fact, for all their anti-sexist rhetoric they were, writes Reynolds, "a rather masculine bunch. They were repressed in ways typical of the hard Marxist left, which fetishised rationality and disdained emotionalism. They extolled hardness and unyielding reason. They also had a quasi-violent stage image, even if they avoided phallic gestures". Instead, they would run around and bash into each other. For such a straight, no-nonsense crew, it was all quite theatrically intense.

Burnham remembers a definite gang-like feeling in the band, with the division of labour between Gill and King, the ideas men, and he and Allen responsible for things like driving the tour van and loading their gear, and travelling to London to elicit interest from journalists, promoters and agents. Even the things that caused tension down the line were, at this point, just another excuse to have a good laugh, like the time Burnham gouged the alert, "Dalrymple means 'Get up late'", down the concrete steps of a basement rehearsal space in honour of Andrew Dalrymple Gill, who, according to the drummer, tended to keep the others waiting.

"We were always hanging around for Andrew," he says, "although even when rehearsals went on quite long and late we'd never go past closing time; that, we were very strict about. The only time I ever saw Andrew Gill run was when someone's watch stopped working and we realised we had only five minutes to make it to the Fenton. When I wrote that thing about Dalrymple it was one of the few times he actually laughed with, not at, someone. Genuinely happy laughter."

Gang Of Four's predilection for alcohol became apparent when they met up with Rockpile in Amsterdam. The old pub-rock booze hounds were managed by the notorious Jake Riviera, who broke the habit of a lifetime when he helped GOF out after their knackered Ford Transit's axle fell off. "He gave us 400 quid to go and get it fixed," says Burnham. "Nobody to this day can believe that Jake Riviera gave anyone money, let alone cash." And fewer can believe that Leeds' radical punk-funk activists were able to keep up with Nick Lowe, Dave Edmunds et al. As Burnham puts it, "All I can say is two generations met their match. Drinking's fun, you know? It's what you do on the road."

It wasn't all fun. Gang Of Four gigs in those days had an air of real danger about them; shows where thugs would, according to Dave Allen, "jump on stage with knives and try and stab us. Even some of our bouncers would just stand back and go, 'No, we're not doing this lot'". Allen recalls a gig at the Electric Ballroom in London's Camden where a huge skinhead, his face and neck covered in swastikas, lunged towards the bassist and proceeded to pull out a knife and puncture the arm of a hapless bouncer. On another occasion they played the Paradiso in Amsterdam, a club run by Hell's Angels, who were by all accounts "completely out of control – they were the judge, the bloody defence and the prosecution". One of them, recalls Allen, had had his face burned away in an incident apparently involving sulphuric acid, leaving him with no nose, just two holes in the middle of his face. Suddenly, this menacing character made his way backstage, where he found a terrified Gang Of Four, and proceeded to pull out bags of "horrible, cheap speed". "It was," says Allen, "like, 'Now we're going to have some fun,' like it was some old gangster movie. It was awful. But there was nothing we could do about it. We were trapped in the dressing room with these guys. Very scary. If my parents had had a webcam of it, they would have thought I was about to be decapitated and thrown in the street."

Another time, in 1978, Jon King found himself the victim of an assault in the band's beloved Fenton after Gang Of Four became a magnet for all manner of violent undesirables. "During '78 there was a change in the perception of us as being in the vanguard of the extreme left," says King, who compares it to when 2-Tone bands Madness and The Specials found themselves with an audience that they neither wanted nor deserved. "But that's what you do when you're young – you fight. And there were quite a few gigs where National Front skinheads would turn up and there would be trouble. The Fenton was assaulted by the British Youth Movement, and a great fight broke out. They came along to have a go, to disrupt everything."

In the melee, King was kicked in the head several times and Andy Gill had his nose broken. "I tried to kick the guy in the nuts who was assaulting Andy, which was a stupid thing to do, and these other two guys got me on the ground and kicked me in the head", recalls King. "I was hospitalised. If you look at my skull there's a little hole where a bundle of nerves came out. It looks like I've had a lobotomy. I was quite ill after that happened, and I still don't have any feeling in my cheek."

In a way, Gang Of Four were like a Clash stripped of all the accoutrements of the romantic outlaw, a Clash without the rebel posturing and tower-block myth-mongering. Gang Of Four were earning a reputation as a "new, improved Clash": agit-punk with a proper grounding in theory.

"I thought The Clash romanticised the whole thing, all that standing with the flag at the barricades in that completely sentimentalised way," says Gill. "It's funny, but Joe Strummer wrote to me once, basically saying, 'the Gang Of Four don't understand, you've got to sweeten the pill. The Clash know how to wrap up the bitter pill, Gang Of Four are just too bitter…' People often go, 'Oh yeah, left-leaning rock band, really exciting live – The Clash, the Gang Of Four.' But we're really dissimilar. I wouldn't say there was much of a pill to swallow with The Clash – don't get me wrong: *London Calling* is fantastic. But the idea that there is tough content being peddled is laughable."

Burnham puts it succinctly: "We didn't really think of ourselves as punk at all. We were a rock group. But we weren't doing old rockist music or old rockist ideas."

It was probably true that the violent incidents at their gigs helped create a bond between the four members of Gang Of Four. Still, even at these, the best of times, Burnham and Allen remember the band dynamic being that of four people more at odds with each other than in sync. A Clash-style Last Gang In Town comprising four like-minded rock'n'roll bad boys they were not.

"We were four very different people," decides Burnham. "It was the same reason that The Who worked so well, because they were four different people pulling in different directions on many things. There were a lot of arguments and fights – and withering remarks. Jon was the one who said what really matters are attitude and ideas, and we had those in spades. Andrew always had the capacity to be very unkind, which was quite frequently – he'd tell people he'd written all my drum parts, which is pretty mean. We were like brothers. And fewer people can be as mean to you or hurt you as much as your brother can."

★   ★   ★

A couple of Gang Of Four gigs from this period in their "career" have now entered band lore. The first was at an art college ball in Carlisle, where their support acts weren't like-minded, socially conscious, post-punk renegades but a racist comedian and a stripper.

"It was funny to see all these art students ogling like crazy," laughs Andy Gill. "No doubt we were doing a bit of ogling as well. So we decided to have a bit of fun with it and turned it into a bit of an event. I can't remember what we were shouting, but we started having a go. Later on she came over to us and said, 'We're both in the entertainment business. Besides, it's better than a nine-to-five job…'"

Jon King can remember exactly what words he chose to interrupt the comic's set and his barrage of racist, sexist jokes. "We started heckling, shouting, 'Fuck off, Adolf!'" Afterwards he came over to us and said, 'Lads, I'm just trying to make a living.' It was interesting that we ruined his set and then had this discussion about why." The band's heated debates with the stripper and comedian would inform the content of the back cover of their first single, 'Damaged Goods'.

They had a no-less instructive encounter after a show in Cumbria, in Dave Allen's home town of Kendal. As Andy Gill relates, the day after the gig, the band were trying to get onto the motorway when they came up against a police blockade, to stop them leaving under the pretence of searching for "stolen televisions". "They were clearly looking for us," he says. "So they took us to the local police station." There, the local drug squad examined the van, and mysteriously "found" a huge lump of dope under the seat that Gill had been sitting in – and, as the guitarist puts it, "I didn't even smoke that stuff."

As a consequence Gang Of Four found themselves incarcerated, albeit briefly, following individual strip-searches. Even Adrian Thrills – the prominent rock journalist who had been sent by *NME* to write a cover story on this amazing new band before they'd even garnered a proper record deal, an unprecedented move on the part of the music paper – was subjected to the humiliating ordeal. "He got busted with us," recalls Andy Gill. "So they took him to a room and got him to drop his trousers and pants, but Adrian couldn't understand the Northern accent, so when this copper told him to, 'Get your knackers up', he thought he meant lift his balls up so they could search there or something."

Hugo Burnham remembers it slightly differently – confusion between the words "knackers" (northern vernacular for under-pants, southern for testicles) and "knickers". "They told him to 'drop your knackers' and Adrian's like, 'Oh, drop my knickers?' So he's standing there and this policeman's saying, 'Put down your knackers, son' and he says, 'But my knickers are down.' And everyone shit themselves laughing." "Being a southerner, he didn't know what the word meant," adds Allen. "He was going, 'You can't do this! I'm a journalist!' I wish we could have filmed the whole thing."

Gill also recalls the hysterical laughter that ensued, although in his case things took a turn for the seriously menacing when, during interrogation, one of the officers pulled back his arm, clenched his fist and moved to punch him after the guitarist denied any prior knowledge of the offending drug substance. "He said something like, 'Nobody talks like that to the Kendal police.'"

By sheer coincidence, the drug squad officer in charge of the operation was an old school acquaintance of Allen's. Not that this earned the band any special treatment. "I said, 'Hey, man. How's it going?' He looked at me and said, 'Shut your mouth, you're in a lot of fucking trouble.'" Allen argues that there is no way the lump of hashish could have been theirs, because "if it had been, we'd have fucking smoked it already." The band was charged, although after one lawyer's strong letter all charges were dropped because, says Allen, "the police didn't have a leg to stand on". Bizarrely, as Allen recounts, the following Christmas his parents moved home, to a house "bang next door to this fucking bastard from the drug squad. There were a lot of black looks over the garden fence."

For Burnham, the Kendal bust was just Gang Of Four business as usual. "Look, everyone did drugs, you know?" he says. "We'd get busted by the police and all that sort of thing. Once they found this bottle of amyl nitrate that had fallen behind the drum case in the van. They just pulled the top off the bottle and sniffed it. It was like, 'What the fuck is that?' 'It's our guitar cleaner.' 'That's fucking horrible, son.'"

According to King, there was a repeat of the Kendal incident later on in Leeds, when some plainclothes policemen strode in to their rehearsal space one day and started rummaging around. "We didn't know they were policemen," says the singer, "so we just said,

'Who are you? Fuck off!' Next thing we know, somebody 'finds' a roach on the floor and before we knew it we were being carted down to the station."

Apparently, Gang Of Four's reputation as subversives was spreading. "There was a lot of panic about Gang Of Four at that time," says King, "and it got pretty hairy. We were banned from going to Portugal because the Pope was visiting and the Portuguese government thought we might cause a riot. I was rather pleased about that one."

The band were all delighted with their first *NME* cover story, especially since the soon-to-be-notorious drug-bust incident made such good copy. But the presence of an as-yet-unsigned band on the front page of Britain's influential music weekly – for a January 1979 issue bearing the cover line: "Four-ward against the forces of reaction and elitism with the Gang Of Four" – caused consternation in some circles. "I don't know if it was Cliff Richard's people or Pink Floyd's people," says Dave Allen, "but someone wrote a letter to the *NME* editor saying, 'You guys are ruining the record industry – how can you possibly have an unsigned band on the cover of *NME*?' Apparently, it was a first. Because we still didn't have a record deal."

★ ★ ★

It was Gang Of Four's opening slot for the Buzzcocks at Ilkley College in November '77 that first drew the attention of the Edinburgh-based indie label that would eventually issue the band's debut EP a year later. Following the Ilkley gig, the band recorded some demos, including 'Love Not Lust', an early version of 'Damaged Goods'. With friend and soundman Rob Warr on board as their first manager, they sent a tape of the demos to Bob Last, whose label, Fast Product, based in Edinburgh, had just released its first record, The Mekons' excellent 'Never Been In A Riot'.

Last was sufficiently impressed to invite the band to release a single on Fast Product. And so it was that, over two days at the end of June '78, Gang Of Four recorded the three tracks that would comprise their debut EP at Cargo Studios in Rochdale. The session was engineered by John Brierley and produced by the band in conjunction with Last himself. An ostensible triple A-side, the EP featured 'Damaged Goods', 'Love Like Anthrax' and 'Armalite Rifle'. The title track was funk meets the Feelgoods, with a powerful two-chord riff courtesy of Andy Gill in full slashing, scything Wilko Johnson mode. An exploration of sexual inadequacy, King yelped hysterically about love as lust while Gill intoned coldly about being soiled by sex, with the title phrase providing the central punning motif: "Damaged goods/Send them back/I can't work, I can't achieve/Send me back/Open the till/And refund the change you said would do me good/Refund the cost...".

'Love Like Anthrax' opened with a monstrous squall of feedback that has been described as sounding "like a man trying to play 'The Star-Spangled Banner' while being electrocuted", before giving way to a loping, tribal beat. Again, King sounded down on love ("I feel like a beetle on its back!") while Gill, out of the other stereo channel, explained the record production process (on the slightly altered version of the song that appears on the band's debut album, *Entertainment!*, the monologue became an attempt to demystify The Love Song in popular music – "I don't think we're saying there's anything wrong with love, we just don't think that what goes on between two people should be shrouded with mystery.")

Dry, sardonic, bleak and industrial, this was a new type of rock music, allied to a new type of rock lyric. As Jon Pareles wrote in *The New York Times*, "King's lyrics are bitterly analytical, infused with theories from Marx, Adorno, Baudrillard and Godard, while the band are determined to puncture pop romance with the consciousness that people are manipulated by power economics, media and marketing." Or, as Simon Reynolds wrote in *Rip It Up And Start Again*: "Inspired by Brecht and Godard's alienation effects, they tried to deconstruct rock even as they rocked hard."

According to Hugo Burnham, 'Anthrax' was inspired, musically at least, by The Velvet Underground's 'The Murder Mystery', nine minutes of droning repetition and disembodied spoken voices that sounded like two people having a dialogue but not really listening to each other. It was all part of GOF's project to play with rock form and content. "We were loud, aggressive and energy-driven," he says. "Our very first few gigs had a punk authority to them, and we loved what you might call ordinary stuff. But it didn't mean we had to ape it. You take something normal and twist it. Isn't that what all art does, art that's interesting? You have to have a starting-off point, and for us that was Dr. Feelgood, Parliament-Funkadelic, dub reggae and Hendrix: you put those four things on the four corners of a square, and then there's us, all careening in the middle, bumping off the sides together."

The final track on the EP was 'Armalite Rifle', a stomping mid-tempo rock song protesting at the army's presence on the streets of Northern Ireland. Again it was left to Gill to dispassionately grumble about this grievous situation, with a bizarrely offhand, drily debunking pay-off line that suggested humour was a far more important element of Gang Of Four's modus operandi than one might have expected, given the accusations of academic joylessness occasionally levelled at the band: "Armalite rifle use it everyday/It'll do you damage it'll do you harm/Blow your legs off blow your guts out/I disapprove of it, so does Dave."

The *Damaged Goods* EP was released on December 10, 1978, and became a number one indie chart hit and John Peel radio show favourite (leading to two outstanding Peel radio sessions) – a great success for Bob Last's new imprint, even if the demand for it caused some tension between band and label. "After they got their confidence and the EP did really well, things got a bit tense", recalls Last. "We'd run out of copies and have to wait six weeks for the next pressing, which they found frustrating. I do know the most successful Fast Product releases were selling in the tens of thousands, which in today's market would put them very high up the charts. We'd have to constantly re-press those Gang Of Four and Mekons records. With The Mekons, Gang Of Four, The Scars and The Human League's 'Being Boiled', we were keeping the pressing plants pretty busy."

Last originally started Fast Product "as a kind of brand" in 1976, with the intention of doing something with it even if he wasn't yet sure whether the brand would be a front for selling music. The only things he was sure about were the "attitude and approach" that Fast Product would have. "The label was informed by a lot of political – small 'p' – thinking," says Last, "so those interests of the band resonated with me. Plus, I'd been listening to Parliament and the funkier Miles Davis stuff, so a lot of what they were doing musically was exciting."

When punk came along, it became obvious that music would be the primary site for Last's ideas. And the first band he got involved with were The Mekons, whom he'd met when they toured with The Rezillos. "So we ambushed The Mekons into recording for us," he recalls, "and that's when they said, 'Are you sure you mean us? Because there's a much better band in Leeds who you should be working with' – and that was Gang Of Four. The Mekons told them to send me something. I remember getting their very early demo tape and loving it."

The demo tape included a couple of songs long since consigned to the vaults (indeed, Last still has them in a vault): a cover of Black Sabbath's 'Iron Man' and a fun little ditty called 'Don't Call Me A Bastard, I'm A Wanker', which Last describes as "very good funk rock." But what shone through most were Gang Of Four's ideas. "As not uncommon then," he says, "bands with these amazing sounds and ideas and world views would pop up almost fully formed. The whole process was pretty quick. The band probably first appeared on our radar in late '77/early '78, but we didn't have to spend months developing them. It was about being instant: 'What you're doing now is great, let's get it out there.' Even the other songs on the demo, which didn't make it onto the EP and were already being left behind by the band, caused us a lot of entertainment and amusement. It was an extraordinary time."

Last considers his role at Fast Product to have been a conduit for GOF's ideas; in the end, band and label lent each other an extra layer of meaning, which created what he calls an "interesting tension" between them. "Because Fast had its own brand and identity, there was a kind of tension, and it wasn't clear who was feeding off of whom, or whether the band were feeding the Fast Product myth. But I'd like to think they were beginning to focus on what classic Gang Of Four was; I'd also like to think I played a part in encouraging that focus."

Although Last enjoyed working with the band, and the *Damaged Goods* EP helped, together with their incendiary live performances, to propel them to international attention and sold-out shows across Europe and North America, it was never his intention to hold on to them or to work with them on a long-player. "Our intention at Fast Product was to bring exciting ideas to people's attention, after which bands would go off," says Last. "We didn't have the capability to make the album. We'd have loved to have made another single or EP with them, but we weren't thinking about albums at that point – we thought they were too time-consuming and boring."

Last fondly recalls, while recording the EP, endless ideological debates about matters both major and minor. "I remember having a debate about reverb on guitar solos and what that did or didn't mean. I'm not sure if Andy's ever forgiven me for putting, on the original solo on 'Damaged Goods', more reverb than there has ever been on his guitar – it was a bit 'rockist'," he laughs. "At Fast Product we had the utmost respect for our artists but we were always a bit playful with them, hence the *Damaged Goods* sleeve, with the letter reprinted on the back cover that they'd sent to me about how they wanted the sleeve to be. It was a sleeve about the sleeve – a meta-sleeve!"

The front cover of the *Damaged Goods* EP was a simple, one-colour affair – crimson – with simple, bold black type. But it was the rear of the sleeve that proved Gang Of Four's credentials in the area of playful ideas-mongering, with hints of situationism and deconstructionism. It featured a tear-out from a newspaper of a female matador spearing a bull, next to which there was an extract from the aforementioned letter that the band had written and sent to Bob Last, bearing full instructions as to how they wanted the sleeve to look and read. "Dear Bob," it went, "enclosed find photographs we'd like to be on the single. The matador is saying, 'You know, we're both in the entertainment business, we have to give the audience what they want. I don't like to do this but I earn double the amount if I were in a 9 to 5 job.' The bull is saying: 'I think that at some point we have to take responsibility for our actions.'"

This was, basically, a word-for-word transcription of the conversations the band had had with the stripper and the comedian at that gig in Carlisle a few months before. "After the Carlisle gig, that's when Jon and I got the idea of using the image with the snippets of that conversation we had with the comedian," says Gill. "It never struck me that I was doing something 'situationist'. We just liked to juxtapose disconcertingly appropriate sources. It [the sleeve] is against the power of the music industry, really."

"I think," says Last, "that they were possibly more leftist and I was more situationist, and that was part of the fun – that's where that playfulness came from. I didn't believe playfulness was the enemy of political impact, and we understood they didn't want to be a straightforward right-on band.

"A lot of the ideas were techniques that Brecht used in the theatre, like on 'Anthrax': Andy's rap about the recording process itself was influenced by Brecht and Walter Benjamin, foregrounding the means of production. But they put these ideas into people's minds. And postmodernism was just coming to the fore and there were a load of critics picking up on these things as exemplars of postmodernism. We loved playing with ideas while simultaneously having these killer riffs pumping away, delivering that visceral thing that pop or rock'n'roll does. That was exciting."

Ever since the advent of punk, and even more so as the post-punk era dawned, people questioned how rock was made and consumed, among them Bob Last himself. "I was interested in how it was consumed – that was a very important part. But then the band decided they wanted to be on a major label, to go into the heart of the beast and play with big marketing power, because they shared that interest in the consumer end of the process."

Last claims to have designed the sleeve himself. "I designed it – but I'm not sure if they liked it! The idea of making the sleeve about the sleeve – that was me. I was feeding off their ideas and their original letter to me." Burnham, however, recalls Gill and King being the designers. "Jon and Andy were the progenitors of the artwork, being art students. They took it, ran with it. There was a situation that came into our life so we made something out of it."

As for the production of the songs, that was mainly Last, although the band get a co-credit. "It was my first production – I'm not sure if I got a credit on The Mekons' 'Never Been In A Riot'. I was very hands-on with a lot of recordings on Fast Product. But really, I was the guardian of the attitude of the label, not a record producer."

There is no doubt about who the prime mover was, ideas-wise. "The internal dynamics of bands are always fascinating," says Last. "When it came to debates about the broader ideas and how they directly impacted on the music being recorded, you tended to have those conversations with Andy more than anyone else."

Gill sees the *Damaged Goods* sleeve as an example of the new, questioning, deconstructivist nature of pop presentation during the post-punk era, an era when record packaging – one thinks of Public Image Limited's cylindrical canister for their *Metal Box* album or the sandpaper inner sleeve of Durutti Column's *The Return Of The Durutti Column* – was used to provoke as much as delight.

Gang Of Four see their destiny on the steps of Leeds Town Hall, 1978. (GEMS/REDFERNS)

Hugo Burnham, aged 7. Bottle of Jack Daniels and neo-Marxist screeds not pictured. **(COURTESY OF HUGO BURNHAM)**

Andy Gill in 1976, taken by Jon King. Don't be fooled by the crop and braces: this was one of the original Ideologically Sound men. **(JON KING)**

Portrait of the avant-funkateer as avant-garde artist. **(COURTESY OF ANDY GILL)**

GoF, Leeds, 1978. "We did enjoy a joke; many a good joke." **(ROB WARR)**

"Hey, hey, we're the GoF-ees!" Leeds, 1978 – taken by manager Rob Warr. **(ROB WARR)**

Andy Gill with Rob Warr in Leeds, 1978, at the
rehearsal studio they shared with The Mekons.
The 'Tom' on the wall refers to Tom Greenhalgh of
The Mekons, and Jolyon is Hugo's brother and the
band's roadie. (**COURTESY OF ANDY GILL**)

Live in 1979, taken by Jolyon Burnham, with Hugo
(front) and Jon on melodica. (**JOLYON BURNHAM**)

Backstage with booze, Germany, 1979. (**COURTESY OF HUGO BURNHAM**)

Andy Gill, Jon King, Dave Allen, Hugo Burnham in Leeds, May 16, 1979. (**VIRGINIA TURBETT/REDFERNS**)

Jon King playing cards on a tourbus in 1979 with members of Pere Ubu on a joint tour Gang Of Four did with Cleveland's finest. (**ANTON CORBIJN**)

Andy and Jon in the Co-Op, during the 1979 GoF/Pere Ubu tour, checking for damaged goods.
(**ANTON CORBIJN**)

At the Hotel Iroquois on West 44th St, NYC. August 1979, in happier times – within 18 months the hotel was the site of Dave Allen's departure from the band. **(FRAN PELZMAN/EBET ROBERTS/REDFERNS)**

Backstage in Brussels, Belgium. February 19, 1980, just before Annik Honore hoved into view.

(PHILIPPE CARLY/NEWWAVEPHOTOS.COM)

The Lennon & McCartney of postpunk funk, live in 1980. (TOM SHEEHAN)

Says Gill, "Prior to that point, you'd had the punk rock sleeve, which was the Clash-style romanticisation of the rock'n'roll era, which we thought was just maintaining the status quo, maintaining the normal rock iconography. For all that's new about punk and what McLaren and Jamie Reid did, all the innovation, it's still presenting a heroic, embattled figure. I always think of Liberty leading the people over the barricade with the wind blowing in her hair, which is definitely where The Clash were coming from. Whereas we loved the jokes – you know, the stripper, the female matador and putting in the stupid speech bubbles of the bull, the farcical nature of it."

While the artwork was fresh, the music, too, ushered in a new era of experimentation and radicalism: *Damaged Goods* was arguably the first post-punk record, although it was surrounded by other strong contenders: Public Image Limited's debut single, Cabaret Voltaire's debut EP, 'Hong Kong Garden' by Siouxsie & The Banshees and Magazine's 'Shot By Both Sides'. Bob Last believes Gang Of Four's debut was the turning point.

"For sure it was *Damaged Goods*, and I'd claim collectively some of the other Fast Product that preceded PiL, Siouxsie or anyone else. Not to take anything away from PiL – that was a very powerful gesture for John Lydon to go in that direction – but the die had already been cast. The postmodern idea of toying with convention in rock music: we claim that." Last, who used to listen to Bootsy Collins and George Clinton records in the Fast Product office, also considers *Damaged Goods* to have been the first example of what has come to be known as punk-funk or funk noir. "The Pop Group and A Certain Ratio were a bit later. Subsequently there was James White & The Blacks in New York, but that conception was Gang Of Four's."

Gill's skeletal, staccato, aggressive guitar has proved an enduring influence. Jon King's threatening on-stage dancing, while equally idiosyncratic, has proved less easy to imitate, although it coincided nicely with Ian Curtis' legendary spasmic dance style. But one of the EP's greatest achievements was that it made politics in pop seem exciting again. As Simon Reynolds has written, "*Damaged Goods* won massive acclaim for its new way of negotiating that thorny danger zone known as politics in rock. It was abrasive but accessible. This wasn't a TRB-style preachy protest or the forbidding didacticism of Henry Cow. It was where radical form met radical content, yet you could dance to it." Reviews for the band around this time began to reach fever pitch: Paul Morley described the band's music as "a kind of demented funk, incredibly white but also, because of political commitment and defiant sloganeering, very dark, and ultimately as close to the depraved edge of the blues as Hendrix."

"We were collectively on a roll, so the EP was received strongly," says Last, who has nothing but fond memories of the period and denies claims by some band members that he underpaid them on the royalty front. "It then went on to perform very well and became a reference point, but my recollection wasn't that it got amazing reviews. Critically it wasn't instantly spotted as a defining recording, even though it carved out its importance very rapidly. The packaging and letter were certainly picked up – I remember in an article about postmodernism in *Harpers & Queen*, by cultural critic Peter York, he cited the *Damaged Goods* and 'Being Boiled' sleeves as exemplars of postmodernist design in pop. So it made its mark straight away. And, of course, in the States, they really enjoyed the hard-core riffing."

Last is amazed by the fascination that his Fast Product releases, especially the *Damaged Goods* EP, continue to exert. But he believes all the acclaim to be well deserved. "We had this amazing run, and it's great to have been a part of it, but I realise now a lot of it was in the ether or the zeitgeist. Nevertheless, we stand by the collective claim to have been first. It wasn't an accident or a fluke – lots of people had been thinking very deeply about the same things: a theoretical analysis of what was going on and how pop and populism worked." Gang Of Four's signal achievement, he concludes, "was to have left a network of influence and provocative thinking that resonates with new generations today. But really, just listen back at phenomenal volume to the record! It was a privilege working with them."

★ ★ ★

Sometime between the release of *Damaged Goods* and the start of the sessions that led to the recording of Gang Of Four's debut album, *Entertainment!*, Jon King – and this was never revealed at the time, or indeed any time afterwards – left the band.

"I said, 'I don't want to be in the band, I want to be an artist'," he says. "I wanted to be a postgraduate at Chelsea or The Royal College or whatever. That's what I'd always wanted to do. I still have regrets to some extent that I didn't carry on doing it. I was totally focused on being an artist. And I was pretty good, you know. I won the Passy Prize and the Windsor & Newton award for Young Painter Of The Year – I had a picture in the Mappin Art Gallery from coming into the finals of that competition."

For King, music was an alternative future. His "core future" was to be an artist. "I didn't want to waste anyone's time, and this wasn't what I wanted to do, so they actually auditioned for another singer. I think Mick Wicksy tried out for it. I left for a couple of months because I didn't want to not take it seriously. The trouble is, you can't be a jack of all trades or a dilettante.

"I thought after *Damaged Goods*, 'You're not bloody doing this for a living,'" he continues. "I felt I'd be letting Andy down particularly because we were very close – he was very much more focused on it, the driving force; he really wanted to make it all happen."

He can't recall the effect his departure had on the rest of the group, nor how the situation was resolved, but, within a few months, King was back in the fold, in readiness for their finest hour. "I'm very vague about it; they must have been distraught, I suppose. I can't quite remember. I don't remember having huge scenes about it or how it all worked out, but I think I got talked back into joining again. I think we had a sort of hiatus. I don't think we did much for about five or six months. And then in my final year at university [1978-79] we did quite a few gigs. We finally arrived in London for the Fast Product night at the Electric Ballroom featuring us, The Human League and The Scars. And everyone was wondering where all these bands came from. From Sheffield? And another one from Leeds? Surely not."

Burnham remembers King's brief absence from the band. "Jon was a fantastic artist, and I think he wanted to go and do a post-grad degree and paint," he recalls. "There was a lot of social pressure for him to move in that direction, and I think he did sort of leave, but it was a bit like, 'Well, OK, let him have his moody. But he'll be back.'"

CHAPTER 4

THAT'S ENTERTAINMENT!

"We wanted to be rubbing shoulders in the ranks with Cliff Richard and Kate Bush." – Andy Gill

"Maybe they were the Velvet Underground of their generation. If you think about the bands that followed them, from Talking Heads and R.E.M. to Franz Ferdinand and Bloc Party, you can smell Gang Of Four in all of their work. They were incredibly influential."
– EMI A&R man Chris Briggs

In 1979, there was a sense of impending megadom about Gang Of Four, the feeling that they could become one of the biggest groups on the planet, the world's first credible stadium band. As Andy Gill puts it, "I know how hard it is for a band to get off the ground, but we went from 0 to 75, if it's out of 100, in six months."

In March of that year, there was a showcase at London's Lyceum Theatre featuring Gang Of Four, The Mekons, The Human League, The Fall and Stiff Little Fingers. It was dubbed The Gig Of The Century, and was rapturously reviewed in *NME* by Charles Shaar Murray, who decided that the concert signalled the start of the Eighties in much the same way that the Fifties began in 1956 with Elvis, the Sixties with The Beatles and the Seventies with 'Virginia Plain', Ziggy Stardust and 'All The Young Dudes'.

In truth, the journalist wasn't entirely convinced by Gang Of Four's set: he viewed it, inexplicably given the presence of SLF, as the most conventional of the night, and was alone among his peers in detecting "nary a hint of Arty Pretension or elitism" about the band. But he did acknowledge their energy and commitment, as well as their ability to mix'n'match genres.

"They leapt on stage with Fenders at the ready," he wrote. "The singer windmilled his arms and shouted, guitarist Andy Gill ran about and waved his guitar and the rhythm section hammered away. They exist on a jagged line drawn between Pere Ubu and Wilko Johnson, with a few reggae detours when they swapped instruments: Gill played drums and the drummer came upfront to blow some melodica in an earnest approximation of Augustus Pablo. They were fine, and the pogoers loved 'em, but definitely late-Seventies. They're a good, contemporary rock band."

Nevertheless, it was Shaar Murray who would later describe GOF as the post-punk Led Zeppelin, such was the almost unearthly force and power of their live attack. Dave Allen believes this was partly due to the way the band were lit on stage: starkly, with no coloured lights, all blacks and whites, the players disappearing into and emerging out of the shadows as they moved around the stage. It all added to the drama and gave Gang Of Four the impact of a much bigger band.

"I've loved him ever since for that!" says Hugo Burnham of the reviewer. "Like Led Zeppelin, we were four very different players and four very different types of people, who were very aggressive in their playing. It wasn't personal aggression but musical aggression, and, again like Zeppelin, we were fairly stripped down. As Charles [Shaar Murray] said, on stage we really did have that power."

"When Shaar Murray said we were the new Led Zeppelin, I was like, 'Pinch of salt. You've got to be joking,'" says Allen. "But then I thought, 'The world is changing, so maybe we could be the big post-punk version of Led Zeppelin.' But we didn't have those illusions. We didn't allow ourselves that arrogance."

Somebody in the Gang Of Four camp who didn't have any qualms about feeling super-ambitious and confident on the band's behalf was their manager, Rob Warr. He had first got involved with GOF while studying at York University. When a friend who'd moved to Leeds told him it was an exciting place to be, he eventually moved there himself. Through The Mekons he met GOF, and soon he became their live-sound mixer. A philosophy graduate, he was, he says, "quite a firebrand socialist", and was aware of the band's influences in that area. "We were," he says, "totally in sync."

But it was their prowess as a live unit that most grabbed Warr. "Live, they were fantastic," he remembers. "Quite incredible. So I was unbelievably excited to be working with them. They were very good musicians, which set them apart from the very primitive punk bands, but they had a chaotic energy. They weren't slick. It was very impressive rock'n'roll. So I did their gigs throughout 1978, then the [Damaged Goods] single came out, they got a lot of attention, and record companies started sniffing round. Suddenly it got serious."

As Warr remembers it, Dave Allen had been the band's quasi-manager, looking after their books and more, but his heart wasn't in it. It was Burnham who proposed that Warr should be their manager, mainly because, according to the drummer, he looked like a manager. "I'm still not sure if it was a compliment or an insult," he says. And so, for an 18-month period between March 1978 and December 1980, Warr either handled their sound or managed them, or did both.

Not surprisingly, given how headstrong and opinionated they were, Gang Of Four were quite a handful. "They were completely impossible to manage," laughs Warr. "They were very smart guys who knew exactly what they wanted, as well as what they didn't want – I was just one voice among five. It was a democratic set-up.

The idea that I was some kind of Svengali who made everyone dance to my tune couldn't be further from the truth. It was a federation of five people. It wasn't a conventional management situation; it was more of a collective, with all the benefits and deficits that phrase suggests."

Warr has particularly fond memories of this period in the band's development, of supporting the Buzzcocks on tour, of travelling between gigs in a Ford Transit and of extraordinary shows like the one at the Lyceum. He remembers the highly charged atmosphere and antagonistic, negative energy when GOF gigs got ambushed by the BNP, but mainly the celebratory mood of the moment. "It was an incredibly exciting time," he says. "Everything exploded, for all of us. They were all in their early twenties, just young men really, as was I – I was exactly the same age as them, so we were all discovering it at the same time. We weren't puritans as we were regarded by some people in the press."

"There was occasional wassailing," jokes Dave Allen of the band's extracurricular acitivities at this point, "but no further than that. We didn't inhale." Gang Of Four, like their contemporaries, Bristol's The Pop Group and Manchester's A Certain Ratio, were pioneers of what became known as post-punk disco – disco for people who didn't wear white suits, disco for people who didn't go to discos, disco for people who didn't necessarily like dancing, nightclubs, or any of the other hedonistic pursuits normally enjoyed by clubbers.

"We did enjoy a joke, though – many a good joke," laughs the bassist. "I remember one tour in America, during the great age of the original arcade games. We stopped at a gas station and there would be rows and rows of these things. And, of course, in clubs where we'd be waiting to soundcheck, there would be the endless thump of these machines – usually it would be Jon playing them, with fans coming up to him, going, 'I can't believe you're playing a video game. It's so capitalist!' And Jon would be like, 'What do you mean? Go away!' They were almost willing us to be these

Marxist, miltant entertainers, although Americans seemed to really get us from the start – we had an amazingly fanatical American fan base."

Andy Gill refutes the idea that he and his bandmates were cerebral neo-Bolsheviks, but he doesn't necessarily agree with their reputation as hard-living lefties, either. As for drugs, they weren't part of the picture – yet.

"There was a combination of those things," he says. "Me and Jon very much liked to talk about stuff like Althussier, you know, but it's a bit of a misconception to imagine we would sit around reading books and discussing them, and then after that writing songs in the light of the conversation. But there was a lot of drink. I'm not sure about drugs – I don't think there was so much coke around in those days – but booze, yes, Your Honour."

With regard to the final part of the sex, drugs and rock'n'roll equation – sex – Hugo Burnham recalls sharing hotel rooms with his brother and band roadie, Jol, and Rob Warr during this period, while Gill, Allen and King shared another (Dave Allen's younger brother Phil was also a member of the road crew). There would be two rooms, then, with one person in one bed and two in the other. "We'd sort of swap and take turns," he says, explaining the system. "It was definitely this sleeping arrangement that provided the catalyst to finding other places to sleep, if you get what I mean…"

Burnham doesn't reveal who was the most successful at acquiring "other places to sleep" each night, but he does add that, whoever got lucky, "it wasn't for the lack of trying on everyone's part." When asked who got the most attention from females, he is adamant: "Well, it wasn't the fucking drummer, OK? It never is. But there were no monks on those tours, apart from Rob Warr, who was particularly virginal – I don't think he'd be embarrassed for me to say that. He was such a good boy. We used to nag him mercilessly about that. But the rest of us – we were in a fucking rock band and we were all in our very early twenties, for fuck's sake."

"They weren't puritanical at all," confirms Rob Warr, who denies that there was any inconsistency between the hard-line anti-sexist gender politics they propounded along with contemporaries Kleenex and GOF associates The Au Pairs, Delta 5, and The Raincoats, and the fun they liked to have on the road. "They liked having ideas about the music and they thought deeply about how to convey them, but they didn't live like monks. Drink was drunk. They were young guys full of passion and testosterone."

"We spent a lot of time stupidly pissed," says Gill, "but when it came to the work we threw ourselves into it 100 per cent. There was no set line on that and it was up to the individual's discretion. Promiscuous sex was had."

It was a lively time all round, Warr remembers. "I recall Andy and Jon getting beaten up in Leeds – Jon had his cheekbone crushed; it was a rough old town back then. They had their fair share of spats, but nothing too big. They were mostly just fighting each other, but it was totally handbags at 12 paces. It never got serious. It was just a fantastically exciting time. Jon and Andy were very, very interesting people intellectually and socially, really good fun; we're still good friends to this day. And I'm very fond of Dave and Hugo. Having a band impact around the world, even on a small scale, is very exciting when you're 22."

"If The Clash were the urban guerrillas of rock'n'roll, Gang Of Four were its revolutionary theoreticians," somebody wrote at the time. Warr believes that, "with a less puritanical, ideological approach," Gang Of Four had the potential to become as big as The Clash. "They were certainly as good a band live as The Clash," he says. He considers them to have been "much purer, less rock'n'roll" than The Clash in terms of their image, or rather non-image, but they had the raw power and sheer energy to deliver their message to an America accustomed to visceral, high-impact, no-nonsense rock'n'roll. In a way, they could have been the polemical, politically charged U2, although, says Warr, "they didn't have the same mindset as U2, or the same ideology. They wanted to be successful, but competely and utterly on their own terms, in a pure artistic way. They were the product of a particular time, when you could get across quite complex intellectual ideas and still make exciting rock'n'roll – that was what made them distinctive. And yet they were completely uncompromising. To be U2 or The Clash you've got to indulge in at least some popular ways of making music. Gang Of Four never wanted to do that. You can't have it both ways."

And yet, for a time, in a sense Gang Of Four did have it both ways: on the one hand, they were the coolest alternative rock band in Britain; on the other, they were about to sign to EMI, a major label and one of the biggest corporations in the music business. It was a move that did little or nothing to harm their credibility. In fact, it was mainly seen as the ultimate subversive gesture – a move right into the heart of the beast that was the music industry, where they could most effectively sustain their "guerrilla-war struggle as the new entertainment", to paraphrase one of their new songs, '5.45', a typically kinetic dance tract about television news.

Gang Of Four's signing to EMI in early 1979, following their indie success with *Damaged Goods* and after being chased by every major label in Christendom ("Everybody wanted to sign us at that point," says Andy Gill), was a coup for both parties. For EMI, they finally had a worthy successor to The Sex Pistols and could right all the things they got wrong with those punk pariahs. As for the band, they now had the freedom and the facilities to spread the word.

As Gill puts it, "They knew they had a terrible reputation in the artistic community because of the Pistols debacle, so they were glad to have a band with credibility on their label, which is why they treated us with kid gloves and let us get on with it. It was a good time to be there." For GOF, this meant total freedom to do as they pleased, without interference. "It was in the EMI contract," he explains, "that we would deliver the finished artwork and records. Nobody interfered. That's the way it worked.

"We wanted to be rubbing shoulders in the ranks with Cliff Richard and Kate Bush," says the guitarist, who didn't see any contradiction in GOF the left-wing, ideologically sound (and therefore, at a guess, anti-militaristic) outsiders being a part of one of the biggest industrial conglomerates in the UK, who traded in everything from entertainment to arms. "It was like a production deal: they gave us the money, we gave them the tapes. We had total control over the packaging and the production of the records. From the beginning, we picked EMI as being a perfect label for us to be on. If we'd been on Rough Trade, it would have been a far less potent juxtaposition."

It was Chris Briggs, formerly a junior A&R scout at Chrysalis and newly ensconced in Manchester Square in EMI's A&R department, who signed the band in early 1979. They were, he says, his "first signing of any significance", the band joining the label's then-roster of cool alternative acts including Dexys Midnight Runners and Wire. Briggs doesn't agree that EMI were keen to make good the damage done by the Pistols. "These things aren't connected. It was a completely new A&R team, with just a couple of exceptions. Whoever had been guilty of the Pistols fiasco was probably higher up, a lot older and wearing a suit. Besides, those people were just scapegoats – it's not as though they would have wanted to drop the Pistols. But that doesn't make such a good story, does it?"

Briggs recalls driving home on the M1 from a gig up north when he heard Gang Of Four being played by John Peel on his nightly Radio 1 show. "It sounds like an absolute cliché, but I heard 'Damaged Goods' on the Peel show, got hold of Bob Last at Fast Product and he gave me Rob Warr's phone number – I drank more than he did, so you might want to check with him! Then I went up to Leeds to see them play. I stayed the night and clicked with them straight away. I really liked them as people – I still do. There was nothing mysterious about the signing process. It was perhaps slightly unexpected that a band like Gang Of Four would sign to EMI, but I was young and naïve and I was just trying to sign the best bands I could. It was a totally different era. The only significant alternative presences were Rough Trade and Mute. Factory weren't coming down south to sign acts – you didn't see Tony Wilson at the Hope & Anchor in 1978 looking for new acts." Briggs didn't see any contradiction in this bunch of so-called neo-Marxist radicals signing to a multinational. "Not really," he says. "If we did, it would have been in an atmosphere of deep black humour. They were very dry."

Gill recalls this being a time when "alternative" bands had endless debates about the pros and cons of independent labels, and would rail against the hypocrisy of indie bands signing to majors. As far as GOF were concerned, the ultimate hypocrisy would have been to sign to an indie. Besides, it wasn't as though being affiliated to a major immediately conferred upon them riches beyond their wildest imaginings – the band paid themselves the grand sum of £30 a week each in those early days at EMI, and they were all living in mostly low-rent accommodation in north London.

"Back in those days, the *NME* and the music press in general, even more than now, used to be always ranting about the independents versus the majors, and how obviously if you went to the majors you'd be giving up vast amounts of artistic freedom, and if you signed to an independent, you know, you'd be gaining huge amounts of artistic freedom. But it's the exact opposite from everything I know from my experiences and everybody else's experiences that I know. You'd be much more likely to have people from the independent label coming along and sitting in on sessions and putting in their opinions. Nobody from EMI ever said anything about anything. They might have come down to the studio, but strictly to buy us a few drinks and tell us a couple of anecdotes. And then they'd go away and we'd get back to work, and once it was finished we'd hand it in: the artwork and the record."

The first record they did hand in to EMI, as a way of "opening their account" in the words of Hugo Burnham, was the single 'At Home He's A Tourist', with 'It's Her Factory' on the flip. It was recorded at the Workhouse Studios in south-east London, where

Ian Dury & The Blockheads' *New Boots And Panties* – "which", according to Hugo Burnham, "we all loved" – was produced. Trumpeted by *NME* as the label's most significant release since The Sex Pistols' 'Anarchy In The UK', the single, issued in June 1979, had that quintessential Gang Of Four approach (abrasive guitar, convulsive rhythm, taut bass pulse), as well as lyrics that looked at the relationship between pop, sex and capitalism and made ingenious pop rhyme out of complex Marxist rhetoric: one's daily life being so conditioned around the employment capitalism demands that, when the day is through, home seems like an alien environment.

Despite the single hardly being the usual chart fodder – as one wag put it, it "stood out like a Trotskyite at the Tory Party conference" – the band's increasing popularity, impeccable credentials and unstoppable forward momentum meant that it was inevitable that they would be invited to perform it on *Top Of The Pops*. Typical of Gang Of Four, the song's lyrics about brusquely corralled teen herds – "Down on the disco floor/They make their profit/From the things they sell/To help you cop off/And the rubbers you hide/In your top left pocket" – managed to comment on the action as it was happening, but it was the reference to condoms that made the BBC jittery, and the band were asked to remove the offending word.

"They objected to the word 'rubbers'," sighs Andy Gill. "Ironic. Now you'd get a medal. They said, 'This is a family show; we can't have you saying rubbers.' So we had a big powwow, and we thought we'd give it a go, so off Jon went and changed it to 'packets', went back into the studio and dropped in the word, and they said, 'Oh no, we want you to change it to "rubbish" so it sounds the same – so it's not obvious that we've censored you.' But it doesn't have the same meaning. At that point I think we said, 'You MUST be taking the piss.' It got pretty acrimonious. Also, we weren't making any proper attempt to mime properly. I'd gotten all the strings on my guitar tied in a knot so they were obviously not being played. I think it was a case of, 'We've got to get this band off somehow or other.' They felt we were a bit too extreme for them."

"Yeah, we decided that we wouldn't move," laughs Jon King. "We would mime really badly and make it really obvious that we were taking a stance." The Beeb promptly decided that GOF's revolution would not be televised, leading John Peel to sarcastically declare: "Obviously we can't have young couples fornicating in front of the television because of Gang Of Four."

As far as Burnham is concerned, the BBC didn't want the band on in the first place, and the "rubbers" farrago was just an excuse. "They used it as an excuse to get rid of us because we refused to play their game," the drummer contends. "We refused to move around during rehearsal. Andy even had all his guitar strings tied in a knot. If we'd been smart, we would have waited until it came time for filming if we really wanted to be rebels, man."

"The producer was really upset with us before he even mentioned the lyrics," agrees King. "But it was total hypocrisy. Number one that week was 'Ring My Bell' by Anita Ward, and we all knew what that was about, yet we can't say 'rubbers'? The worst part of it was that by us pulling out, it let in Dire Straits, who got to do 'Sultans Of Swing' on *Top Of The Pops* thanks to Gang Of Four. We launched their career, which isn't something to be too proud of. When I die I can see myself at the gates of heaven with St Peter saying, 'Well, on the one hand you've been a good man, on the other – 'Sultans Of Swing'. Sorry, downstairs, mate!'"

Burnham doesn't believe it was Dire Straits who replaced GOF – "That," he says, "is an urban myth. It was someone like Sniff & The Tears, a pub-rock band – I'd bet my life it wasn't Dire Straits." That aside, at the time, the band, who had been playing in Holland and had to fly back quickly for the TV performance, were all united that they were doing the right thing.

Unfortunately, the net result of their refusal to cooperate with the BBC was that the single stalled at number 58, and Gang Of Four's first crossover moment had passed. What might have seemed to some a heroic gesture today looks like a missed opportunity.

"We really did fuck up our forward movement when we walked

off *Top Of The Pops*," says Burnham. "Not so much for the public – most of them hadn't even heard of us, which would have changed – but for EMI. The head of radio promotion was like, 'I can't believe this.' You could almost hear the building say as one: 'All right then, fuck you.' It was a shame. The *NME* thought we were cool for the next few weeks, and John Peel came out and supported us, but what it ultimately did was fuck us for the BBC and for EMI. They'd been supporting us really hard, working their bollocks off to get us on the show, and that's how we repaid them. Frankly, you could say it was career suicide."

Ironically, as the band's friend and journalist Mary Harron has argued, King could have sung "rubbish" all along because the song explains how non-stop circulation of cultural commodities robs people of their leisure time. In fact, the incident has been cited as an example of the band's naivete, and that's without even mentioning the deleterious effect it had on record sales at a crucial point in their career. Chris Briggs found the whole *Top Of The Pops* affair "absolutely farcical".

"We'd done the camera run-through, the people at *TOTP* had the record, we'd had a rehearsal and they hadn't spotted anything they didn't like," he says. "I was there on the studio floor and my memory of it is that a young woman, wearing a dress that Princess Anne might have considered old-fashioned and holding a clipboard, told us we were no longer required. At first we thought it was a joke. We didn't realise she was being serious. But the band didn't really want to change [the word]. It was very bizarre. I tried to talk to the producer – he'd previously been the producer of *The Basil Brush Show*. I tried to plead our case but I didn't succeed. So we went to the BBC club instead and got very, very drunk. Did they lose commercial momentum? Absolutely."

★ ★ ★

Fortunately, Gang Of Four had another card up their sleeve, and it just happened to be one of the greatest debut albums – one of the greatest albums period – in rock history: *Entertainment!* Over a dozen tracks, the album made life-altering magic out of a bleak anti-pop world view, heightened by the thrill of being allowed to do this by EMI.

In between April 1979, when they went on Rock Against Racism's massive Militant Entertainment tour, which featured 30 bands including GOF, The Mekons, The Ruts, The Specials and Stiff Little Fingers, and August's Rock Against Sexism gig at London's Electric Ballroom, featuring GOF and Delta 5, the band worked on their debut album. After spending three weeks in Wales in a hippie enclave, demoing songs and writing a couple of new ones, they decided to return to the Workhouse, having enjoyed making 'At Home He's A Tourist' there. The album took five weeks to record, during which time the band lived on a houseboat in Chelsea. "It was fun waking up at funny angles when the tide had gone out," recalls Burnham.

Rob Warr co-produced *Entertainment!* Although he enjoyed the experience, he would never produce again. "It wasn't the discipline I wanted, spending weeks in a dark studio listening to drum loops. You need tunnel vision to be a good producer." Chris Briggs also got quite involved in the recording process. "Some A&R men don't go down to the studio at all, but those of us interested in recording would spend a lot of time there. Maybe I'm just nosey. But they were a very interesting group of people, and they didn't mind me being there. I was completely in love with the band so I had no objectivity."

With a clear idea of how they wanted the album to sound in their heads, the band chose not to have an outside sonic arbiter, even though Martin Hannett, Joy Division's producer, was, according to Gill, in the frame. Instead they twiddled the knobs themselves, along with Warr and Rick Walton as engineer. Briggs remembers the minute attention to detail brought to bear by the band during recording. "There was a lot of deep analysis about the recording process, all the traditional ways of recording," he says.

"Even the use of tape delay on vocals would require two hours in the pub of very intense discussion. Any common practice was deconstructed and reconstructed, not taken for granted. It was quite entertaining – and made you question everything. Andy in particular would question everything very rigorously, and it made you understand why you wanted to do things in a certain way."

Gill, King, Warr and Walton gave *Entertainment!* a spare, driving sound. As Simon Reynolds wrote in *Rip It Up And Start Again*, the album was "a studio artefact, a cold-blooded construction, sober, flat, remote, in your face, dry, with no reverb [a sound that was achieved by dangling a microphone in the studio toilet]. It wasn't live-sounding. It was dry emotionally, too: using the scalpel of Marxist analysis to dissect the mystifications of love, 'capitalist democracy' and rock itself. Relationships and situations were depicted diagrammatically. It saw through false consciousness to the structural realities that govern our existence."

Burnham enjoyed being back in the Workhouse: "We liked the vibe of the place," he says, although he remembers just before recording *Entertainment!* suffering from "terrible red light fever". "It was a sort of two-storey room and everyone would be looking down at you from the sides. Dave and I did our parts first, and I just remember being so tense, sort of, 'This is it. This is the record', you know? There were all these expectations and all this talk about us being the Second Coming or whatever."

More tension arose as a result of the band's much-touted democratic set-up proving to have been more of an ideal than a reality. "Dave and I really didn't get involved in the production side of things, largely because there was nowhere to sit in the studio. All the good seats were taken. It was very annoying, because you just felt like, 'Oh Christ, nobody's really listening'. There were too many cooks in there."

Warr remembers things differently. "Production, like management of the band, was a democracy. It was all of us," he says, although he does concede that "it was very much driven by Andy and Jon's songs, with everyone else chipping in. The others contributed, but Jon and Andy were the creative heart – they were unequal partners. It must have been tough for Dave and Hugo because Jon and Andy had known each other since they were 12, so their bond was much stronger than the rest of the band."

According to Burnham, the band would "argue like fuck over things." He remembers one row in particular with Warr. "I got into a real screaming match with him, and he's quite a bit taller than me, and I just said, 'Well, fuck off. I'll give you a fucking fat lip!' And as I said it I felt like such an idiot. And he laughed at me, as I deserved. You know, deflated completely. It was like, 'Oh, fuck it, there's no point getting involved in any of this.' I don't think there was ever a real fight between us. There was lots of moody aggression, and meanness, but the only real out-and-out fisticuffs didn't come till 2006… The arguments were mostly musical, about hi-hats and stuff, or whether people were playing too much."

What would a fly on the wall have seen during those sessions for *Entertainment!*? "It probably would have been quite brutal," says King. "We weren't very nice to each other. Really quite horrible, in fact. Andy and I liked being with each other. But it was all about testing it, testing it, testing it." The sessions were "hard work but great", says Warr. Gill, he recalls, got "quite ill" with "gut rot of some sort – he was a delicate lad and susceptible, but other than that it was a joy. It was great to get all those songs captured. It was an exciting time, although I had no idea it would have as long a life as it's had. It's quite extraordinary, really. What's interesting is that we were very, very insistent that we record it our way. There was no record company involvement or demands for changes, which was quite unusual at the time."

EMI were just relieved to have a credible band and a credible record. "They didn't have over-expectations", says Chris Briggs. "It didn't go gold, but it did respectably. It wasn't a breakout record. But then, I knew after the *TOTP* 'rubbers' incident that it was always going to be much more of a cult thing."

The title of *Entertainment!* was inspired by that pivotal Carlisle incident involving the comedian and the stripper. The album expounded upon "the problem of leisure" and the lie of consumer culture ('Return The Gift'), its broad, socio-political sweep also touching upon the media ('5.45'), the arms trade ('Guns Before Butter'), advertising ('I Found That Essence Rare'), sex as deal-making ('Contract'), even the torture of suspected terrorists ('Ether').

Against formidably tough competition from post-punk's premier league – PiL (*Metal Box*), Joy Divison (*Unknown Pleasures*), The Pop Group (*Y*), The Slits (*Cut*), Magazine (*Secondhand Daylight*), Talking Heads (*Fear Of Music*) and Wire (*154*) – *Entertainment!* made number five in *NME*'s albums of the year. During the recording of the album, however, the band weren't remotely aware that they were making a masterpiece, a stone-cold future classic.

"Not at all," says Burnham. "You always go in thinking you're going to do something fantastic. But it would be ridiculous for anyone to say, 'Yes, we were really trying to break down barriers...' We just knew we wanted to do things differently. We had a punk ethic – as few overdubs as possible because we wanted it to be real. We didn't want to overtreat it, and it rather went too far the other way, in retrospect. For example, I wanted the drums to sound a bit bigger, and that wasn't going to happen. I didn't want the drums to sound quite so much like cardboard boxes being bashed."

For Rob Warr, "On *Entertainment!*, there isn't a word that isn't on-message or that resorts to rock'n'roll cliché. Their purity marks them out." GOF's rigorous approach to everything they did extended to their music press interviews. Dave Allen remembers journalists being quite in awe of the band. "I think part of the Gang Of Four history has been a series of missteps by the media," he considers. "A lot of the journalists weren't intelligent enough to deal with Jon and Andy when they were at the top of their game. Many of them were clearly out of their depth. The writers would ask a question and 15 minutes later they were like, 'Oh, er, and what's your favourite colour?' Nobody talked like this in rock'n'roll interviews."

Not that Gang Of Four had become, by this stage, any more po-faced or pretentious than before, nor had they allowed all the acclaim they were then getting to go to their heads. "They were taken uniquely seriously," says Chris Briggs, "but they weren't uniquely serious people. If they were radical neo-Bolsheviks, they were very witty and entertaining, hard-drinking radical neo-Bolsheviks. They were very bright people. Their commentary on their own career was always spot-on and highly entertaining. Jon was very good at putting things into a snappy sentence when things were looking gloomy. Of all the bands I've worked with, and I've been doing this for a fuck of a long time, these are some of my fondest memories."

"We weren't really Marxists," reassures Gill. "Sometimes we could seem a bit austere but, from the name onwards, there was an enormous amount of humour in it, real dark humour, real belly laughs. Gang Of Four were never about hoisting the big flag and saying, 'Comrades, let's go for it!' But songs like 'At Home He's A Tourist' and 'Natural's Not In It' demonstrated everything we *were* about. That feeling that people aren't really in control of their own lives, the realisation that there are unseen constructs of a ruling elite. 'The problem with leisure: what to do for pleasure?' That's the aching cry of someone whose only outlet is consumerism."

King's lyrics gave the band an air of mystery, ironic considering their attempts to demystify everything from love to the recording process itself. *Entertainment!* presents the world as "a Matrix-like product of false consciousness", writes Simon Reynolds; "that even our most personal choices – love, sex, leisure – are hallucinations, products to be bought and used."

"I would try to write in plain English but English that was twisted in some sort of way," explains King. "I didn't want a bunch of bad rhymes like some fucking Hallmark Christmas card – so I would often rhyme words with the exact same word. Or I'd use assonance: 'He fills his head with culture – he gives himself an ulcer [from 'At Home He's A Tourist'].' I didn't like the idea that you went around like the *Readers Digest* and had to learn a new word every day. So I was trying to write simply but then invest it with meaning. It was really serious. The words have authenticity. What characterises great music – and I'm not saying that we did produce great music – is that it's got authenticity. We did not make music to make money. Full stop. Now you've got the banal observation that every band's got an invisible accountant as their fifth member."

On *Entertainment!* King declaims brittle sentiments in a demagogic sing-speak voice – a fusion of John Lydon's Sex Pistols snarl, a conversational drone and feverish pulpit barks – as Allen, Burnham and Gill churn up a brutal, sparsely embellished accompaniment of Gatling-gun guitar chords and snowballing bass and drum patterns. "Allen's explosive bass and Burnham's deft command of funk, reggae and revved-up disco meters form a one-two punch whose tactility and musical strength equals that of the Stones and the Wailers," wrote one startled reviewer. "Gill ignores routine rock-guitar riffing, preferring instead to fire off polyrhythmic volleys of crackling dissonance that have more in common with Wilko Johnson than Johnny Ramone."

There were manic James Brown mutations ('Not Great Men') and implosive three-chord rock'n'roll ('I Found That Essence Rare'); even the dour rationalisations about love and sex in 'Damaged Goods' (re-recorded in a faster and more furious form for the album) and 'Contract' had stinging riffs and propulsive, ricocheting rhythms that were like Captain Beefheart's Magic Band trying to play Lee Perry. This was a new kind of rock'n'roll: the urgency of lo-fi punk, the danceability of funk and African rhythms, the mesmeric qualities of dub, and the grit of old-fashioned R&B.

"Like a goose-stepping Led Zeppelin or a lusty Plastic Ono Band," as another reviewer gasped. "They can just as easily work up a funky Parliament-Funkadelic sweat or slip into a psychotic stream of echoed PiL-like dub." You could listen and dance to *Entertainment!* Like PiL, The Pop Group, A Certain Ratio and Talking Heads, GOF had invented a new type of dance music: "death disco", as PiL had it.

The new type of dance music evinced on *Entertainment!* was unnaturally tightly constructed, almost with scientific precision, and eschewed improvisation. 'Anthrax', for example, was based on a deliberately monotonous drum and bass loop that lasted for several minutes but featured no cymbal crashes or fills – none of the standbys of rock drummers. "It's got very clean lines," points out Gill, whose penchant was for a cold analysis of everyday situations. "I liked to examine the artifice within things – that was something we kept going back to. 'Natural's Not In It' is about what is natural and what isn't, what is learned and what's invented. It's about looking at the structures behind the surface of everyday life to see what makes everything tick. On 'It's Her Factory', we asked whether it was natural that the woman stays at home while the man goes out to work. In the Fifties and Sixties it was considered the natural thing but now it's not."

Between post-punk and the New Pop of the early Eighties, there was a remystification of love and romance. Punk dismissed sex as "two minutes of squelching noises"; post-punk was the transitional, coldly analytical phase. In GOF's world, love was at best a business partnership ('Contract'), at worst a disease ('Anthrax'). So why were Gang Of Four so down on love? "We weren't down on it," laughs Gill. "We just thought it was nonsensical to try to pretend it was [perfect]. We had these images of the bedroom as a sexual laboratory, not some furry, pink, cosy space. Love songs always choose to separate love out as being a special event unconnected to economics. We weren't ambiguous, like so many other people who aren't quite sure what they're trying to say. We'd worked out what we wanted to say by the time we started work on the record."

As a result of *Entertainment!*, Gang Of Four were subject to degree-level scrutiny, with the band as arbiters of a new socio-political consciousness. There was pressure on King and Gill, particularly, to make sense of the world. "We were being asked in every interview: 'How does this change the world exactly?'" says Gill. "Jon and I certainly read things by post-Marxist people like Walter Benjamin and Althussier, partly as a result of what we were doing in fine art, but really it was just about challenging the idea of what's natural. 'The personal is political' was the phrase of the day, and we were talking about the politicisation of daily life. 'He'd Send In The Army' – in no way is it criticising this fictional character in the army. It's just using somebody as an example, and wondering how he thinks. He gets his orders from his superior in the army and carries out those orders, then gives his pay cheque to his wife, who then pays him back in the bedroom. It looks at the web of economic, sexual and political relations in controlling forces. We were exploring the relationship between ourselves and our actions. Not that I considered myself in any way an ideologically sound individual who should be copied. Christ, no. I'm not a role model."

Nevertheless, Gill acknowledges the importance of the work the band were doing. "I certainly felt that *Entertainment!* was important. I felt that we'd changed things a bit, that we'd moved the game on a bit from the Pistols, even The Slits. I didn't feel that we had much in common with other bands, even The Pop Group, whom we were always being compared to. We had a greater clarity of thought, whether you agreed with what we were thinking or not. We weren't trying to be mystical or mysterious. I feel we have slightly failed if you have to do background reading. Personally, I hadn't read a single word of Beaudrillard. What we were doing wasn't intellectual; it was from the gut, like painting a picture. All the ideas – the riffs and the beats – you don't have to try to understand them. Every relevant aspect of Gang Of Four is understandable whether you have O levels or not. 'Anthrax' is just feedback, with a drum and bass loop that doesn't change, with Jon singing and me commenting on the idea of a love song. That's it. Simple, really."

Dave Allen admits that, despite not having much involvement with them, he was "in awe of how brilliant the lyrics were, the way they talked about the commodification of the individual". King's own personal favourite song was 'He'd Send In The Army', which became known as 'The Microwave Song' because he latterly would bash a microwave oven with a stick on stage. "But that wasn't the point of it," he explains. "The lyrics are about this bloke at home and he's a bit of a bully, and he wants his family to obey him like he obeys his bosses. It's brilliantly ludicrous and I thoroughly enjoyed it. It's extreme."

The sleeve, as much as the words and music, was a bold statement in itself. Bright red, with blue and yellow lettering, it featured cartoon images of a "cowboy" and "Indian" (which King found in a Belgian TV guide) and bore the words: "The Indian smiles, he thinks that the cowboy is his friend. The cowboy smiles, he is glad the Indian is fooled. Now he can exploit him." The album's ideas were neatly, pithily expressed. "Me and Jon had very strong ideas about the sleeve," says Gill. "We didn't want it to look like anything else, and it was very much part of the way we wanted to project ourselves." Chris Briggs regards the *Entertainment!* sleeve as part of EMI's rich heritage of radically unusual front cover designs. "Jon painstakingly explained why the red and blue together would stand out miles away in a shop window. It was brilliant. But remember: EMI had the Harvest label, Pink Floyd, Roy Harper and the Third Ear Band, so there was already a culture of flying pigs on album covers with no photos of the band, although it is seen as a staid organisation. People forget that Wire were on EMI!"

At the time, nobody had any idea that the album would prove so enduring, and so influential. For Briggs, even given the slew of landmark albums released that year, *Entertainment!* stands out. "In many ways it's first. It's a more radical piece of work. A record that a lot of people listened to subsequently." As for Jon King, he denies any sense of competition with their post-punk peers. "Obviously we had things in common with them but I wasn't really aware of Joy Division or those other bands. [Talking Head's] *Fear Of Music*, yes, that was a great record. You hear things and take it on board but not in the sense of, 'That is brilliant, we must do something better than that.'"

The shockwaves caused by *Entertainment!* were felt immediately. Paul Weller wrote 'That's Entertainment' in the wake of *Entertainment!*, while The Jam's 'Going Underground' had a decidedly Gill-esque scything guitar sound. Which was more than mere coincidence, as far as Gill is concerned. "Paul Weller really admired Gang Of Four. I remember we played with The Jam in north London, at the Rainbow, and for some reason they were supporting us. I think Weller thought we were doing better than we actually were in America in terms of sales and stuff, and The Jam always had a hard time there. He kept questioning me backstage about America. 'How did you do this? What have you done there?'"

The album's long-term effect was even greater. It wasn't just disenfranchised British youths or cerebral UK students who were paying attention to GOF's radical new sound: Kurt Cobain of Nirvana, Flea and Anthony Kiedis of Red Hot Chili Peppers, Michael Stipe and Peter Buck of R.E.M., prime movers on the US hardcore scene such as Henry Rollins and Steve Albini – they were all paying close attention. "Kurt Cobain was a mad fan of *Entertainment!*" says Gill. "So were Tad Doyle and Dave Grohl. In fact, Tad had this covers band called Red Set that just played *Entertainment!*"

Many of GOF's fans have paid tribute to the band in print. On the sleeve of the 1995 CD reissue of the album, Flea wrote: "Gang Of Four is the first rock band I could relate to, the first to make me want to go crazy and dance and fuck and feel like I was part of something really cool… It made me laugh to hear the guy from

U2 talk about his guitar influences being old bluesmen. I thought, 'Hey, you dipshit, what about Andy Gill?' The groove laid down by the Burnham-Gill-Allen-King connection on 'Not Great Men' is the first thing I put on my turntable to show somebody what shaped the sound of the rookie Red Hot Chili Peppers." On the same CD sleeve, Tad Doyle confirmed what was suspected – "*Entertainment!* changed my life. It did for Kurt Cobain, too" – while Michael Stipe simply stated: "*Entertainment!* shredded everything that came before it. The Gang Of Four know how to swing. I stole a lot from them."

No amount of record sales can buy that kind of acclaim. And yet, as far as EMI were concerned, *Entertainment!* should have sold more. Chris Briggs was disappointed by the album's failure to match critical acclaim in the marketplace. It fell short of the label's, and the band's, aims for mass-market penetration. "I signed them because I thought they were absolutely fantastic and loved the songs," he says. "If they'd been paid by the five-star review, they'd have been very rich men. For whatever reason, they connected with critics and musicians more than the public. But I did think *Entertainment!* would do much better than it did. I was very disappointed – not artistically but commercially. Maybe they were the Velvet Underground of their generation. If you think about the bands that followed them, from Talking Heads and R.E.M. to Franz Ferdinand and Bloc Party, you can smell Gang Of Four in all of their work. They were incredibly influential."

One of those five-star reviews appeared in *Rolling Stone* magazine. Wrote David Fricke: "*Entertainment!* isn't just the best debut album by a British band – punk or otherwise – since the original English release of *The Clash* in 1977. Nor is it simply a fierce, emotionally taut dramatisation of youth's loss of innocence as seen through the clouded lens of neo-Marxist dogma and ambitiously obscure free verse. Stripped of its own pretensions and the burden of sociopolitical relevance forced on it by a knee-jerk leftist English music press, *Entertainment!* is a passionate declaration of discontent by four rock'n'roll agents provocateurs naive enough to believe they can move the world with words and music. It's also the first real political partying record since the MC5's booty-shaking 1969 broadside, *Kick Out The Jams*."

Credibility and acclaim aside, there remains the distinct feeling that Gang Of Four should have been bigger on the back of *Entertainment!*, and that the world would have been somehow a better place with them bestriding it like neo-Marxist funk-rockin' colossi. The impression given by Chris Briggs is that more should have been done to promote and market the band, notwithstanding the irony of trying to sell music that was itself, in one way, about the selling of entertainment. "I left EMI because the people at the very top were frustratingly difficult to deal with," says Briggs. "They were absolutely clueless. I would have spent more money on marketing and drawn more attention to the band. I do think they're 'the one who got away'. But unlike, say, U2 or The Police, they didn't change into anything to get signed. It was there, take it or leave it. There were no compromises. I thought of Gang Of Four as like those classic big rock bands who didn't have hit singles, like Led Zeppelin, who were driven by the quality of their material and performance, and could build a big fan base live, which it was still possible to do in the late Seventies."

There were no parties to celebrate the release of *Entertainment!* in September 1979, there remained just a sense of a great job having been done and the next move needing planning. "We were pretty basic," says Rob Warr. "We probably went to the pub and got utterly pissed. We played snooker a lot – Andy's a good player. We were pretty proletarian in our celebrations. There were no set-piece excessive rock'n'roll parties this time."

CHAPTER 5

AMERICAN GANG-STERS

"We were rock stars who were anti-rock star. Nothing was really that self-conscious when we talked about it and thought about it. It was just, like, to be in a good rock band you don't have to be a dickhead, something I think a lot of people appreciated." – Hugo Burnham

Perhaps in a bid to sustain their momentum, maybe simply because the band was on fire at this point, Gang Of Four undertook a 12-week tour of the United States in between recording *Entertainment!* and its release in the UK in September 1979. They may have already signed to EMI after having been chased by most of the major British record companies – with the exception of Island, who turned them down, much to the band's chagrin, who quite fancied being on the label that brought the world Free and Bob Marley – but they had yet to ink an American deal. They knew that whoever they signed with in the US, it would, as with their deal at home, be with a major.

As Hugo Burnham says of their EMI contract, "Who were we going to go with? Rough Trade? What we were doing was important, we wanted lots of people to see it, hear it, and the potential for doing that was greater with a better business machine behind us." In addition, as he explains, they saw the big record companies as places that would allow them greater artistic freedom, which was more important to the band than spending money. "We took a third of the money the other labels were offering us to go with EMI in return for complete artistic control," he says. "We didn't have clauses whereby the label could decide [that] what we did wasn't commercially acceptable. As long as it was technically releasable they had to accept the tapes, the delivery of whatever we gave them. We didn't take a lot of money but we got a higher royalty rate."

In the end, they went with Warner Brothers in the State after a bidding war as fierce as the one back home six months before. "Rob would call up labels, telling them to come and see us – he'd say, '*Entertainment!*'s a great record, but live they're insanely powerful,'" says Dave Allen. "Once they'd seen us they'd start bidding."

As for the cash money they now had to live on thanks to EMI, their salary was the princely sum of £30 a week each – that is, the four GOF members, plus manager Rob Warr and the two road crew, Hugo's younger brother Jol and Dave Allen's kid brother Phil – plus a "per diem" (daily pocket money) of around £10. In fact, it was the per diems that provided further impetus for their decision to go on the road in the States.

"We said, 'Let's get on the road and make another £10 a day in per diems' – I think it was £12 or maybe eight." Burnham remembers the amount going up to about £50 a day after a while, and after a couple of US tours they personally recouped "a couple of grand each – but there was never any real money around." Instead, the four invested in the band's future – for example, in lighting rigs that would mean no longer having to rent such gear. "It was sound practice, and it gave us control, it gave us a stake in something. But no," Burnham confirms, "there was never lots of money."

And so it was that, in August '79, having just completed their brilliant debut album, Gang Of Four headed to America for a tour booked by FBI management's Ian Copeland, brother of The

Police's manager Miles. "We went over there self-financed and we actually came home with about £400 or £500," says Burnham. He remembers their US tour van – previously used by either The Police or Squeeze, Burnham can't quite recall – being dropped off at their New York hotel on a Friday afternoon, at which point the band loaded all their equipment into it and set off for Philadelphia, only for it to break down in a midtown tunnel. The previous occupants had, as a wizard wheeze, filled the petrol tank with something incompatible "to fuck with us". GOF took it well. "We were all laughing drunk, even though Rob was like, 'No!' But it was a great tour; great fun. We had three bedrooms, two to a bed."

Their tourmates on the American dates were the Buzzcocks, but it was Gang Of Four who were the stars of the shows. "We were an enormous critical hit," says Burnham. "I love listening to the live stuff – it's the truest form of what we were doing."

One gig stood out for both the band and American audiences: the intensely hot summer night at the Geary Temple in San Francisco. "I'm not being self-aggrandizing when I say all of the gigs were great, but that was the highpoint, emotionally, for me. It was the hottest night in the city for about 20 years. The place had a 1,600 capacity, but there were well over 2,000 people in there. It was cripplingly hot and crammed. Expectations were running high. It was just... monumental. Robert Fripp talks about the moment when you're playing and it's almost like an out-of-body experience, when you're so transported beyond yourself that you stop thinking about what you're playing, and then anything you play becomes seamless, perfect, almost orgasmic – and we hit that as a band that night. You can rise up and see everything that's going on, where everything's going, anything you're going to try you just know will work, and you're in that space where it's like, 'Oh my God, the audience is great, we're great, the on-stage sound is great...'" That SF gig, says Burnham, changed people's lives. "People – musicians, managers, journalists – talk to me about it more than anything I've done in my career. Stan Ridgway from

Wall Of Voodoo, Romeo Void, Flea from the Chili Peppers – they were all there. We loved playing together. All the other stuff went out the window."

Andy Gill agrees that the American response to GOF's live fury was one of gobsmacked rapture, especially when, during 'He'd Send In The Army' – a disquisition on militarism and fascism that later formed part of the untitled, so-called 'Yellow EP' UK single – Jon King started slowly hitting an old fridge with a metal pole like it was a metronome, while Gill unleashed howls of feedback with his guitar before Burnham and Allen piled in. "Audiences were open-mouthed – nobody had seen or heard anything like it," says the guitarist, who points out that, later on, R.E.M. would include a version of '… Army' in their live set.

One notable awestruck punter at that Geary Temple gig was renowned American music writer Greil Marcus, author of *Mystery Train*, *Lipstick Traces* and *In The Fascist Bathroom*, who famously left before the Buzzcocks arrived on stage because he didn't want anything to detract from the moment. "I have overwhelmingly vivid memories of that gig," he says. "It was one of the most striking shows I'd ever seen. I just walked away transfixed. It was so dramatic and so scary that, when it was over, I didn't want anything to interfere with the sense of doom and struggle that seemed to have been projected from the stage. So I just left and went for a long walk in San Francisco to try and absorb what I had seen. And I kept thinking of these Last Man Standing British movies – war movies or sci-fi movies – because the way Andy Gill stood on stage reminded me of that posture. It was doomed heroic. That's what I fixed on."

After GOF's performance – "one of the most dynamic and draining physical performances anyone's ever done" – Marcus remembers heading back to the dressing room area, only to look over his shoulder at the stage and realise that none of the band had yet left the stage. Instead, they were "laid out on chairs, barely conscious, exhausted".

Marcus saw GOF live before he heard *Entertainment!* After that, he would give copies to friends he assumed would enjoy it. Problem was, "they thought it was totally unlistenable, weird art music, not rock'n'roll. They didn't want anything to do with it. A lot of people reacted that way, maybe because there was too much thought in the music. I like the sound of people thinking, and not everybody did.

"I saw the band before I heard the records," he adds. "I didn't know who they were, I hadn't heard their music, so I came to it completely cold, and I walked away shaking my head: 'Who are these people?'"

Marcus didn't necessarily see Gang Of Four, as many commentators did, as the next logical step after The Sex Pistols – "I didn't think of it in those terms," he says – although he did see them as "speaking the same language. They were working with the same freedom of invention and discovery that the Pistols opened up for so many people." For him, GOF represented both a break with, and a continuation of, rock tradition. More than anything, they left him feeling disoriented. "What was so thrilling about the Pistols and The Clash was it was something I'd never heard before. I didn't understand why they were so powerful and why the power seemed different from other rock'n'roll. Something different was going on here. And I had the same feeling with Gang Of Four: that same feeling where the ground under my feet is not really stable. There was that same sense of displacement and uncertainty that I found so delicious with the Pistols and The Clash."

Evoking what Allen and Burnham have said about the band comprising four individuals pulling in different directions, Marcus says, "They did, on stage, shoot off in different directions, but somehow they held it together – that's why they were so exciting." So exciting, in fact, that there was no earthly reason why they shouldn't appeal to an American audience. Marcus never regarded GOF as too British for US crowds to make the necessary connections. "'Return The Gift' was [sufficiently] radio-friendly [for the States]. They were a modern band, about the modern predicament, about alienation and existential dread and how to think about that stuff, or how to dramatise or bring it to life for ordinary people," he says. "They don't seem as British as The Mekons do to me. There is a folk strain in The Mekons to do with searching for ancestors and precursors, and seeing them in the 19th and 15th centuries. That sense of being wedded to a history. Whereas Gang Of Four are much more French in terms of their sensibility. Their radicalism comes from an apprehension that grows out of ordinary life."

Burnham concurs: "Our concerns weren't British in that we didn't go around singing songs about Margaret Thatcher this and National Front that. The themes were – and I hate to use this phrase – universal. It was more about – I hate this expression as well – the politics of the self, expressing yourself and investigating your own thoughts and ideas, and that applied to anyone. It didn't matter where you were from. And we were a kick-ass, steaming rock band. And we had fun. We were fun *and* funny. This band had massive wit about them. And when you have people who are that good, and they're interesting, it comes off on stage."

Americans, Burnham says, got off on GOF's healthy self-deprecation. "We were rock stars who were anti-rock star. Nothing was really that self-conscious when we talked about it and thought about it. It was just, like, to be in a good rock band you don't have to be a dickhead, something I think a lot of people appreciated."

Marcus was never fazed by GOF's penetration of the US market. Apart from their sense of humour, it was their very smartness and radicalism that appealed to America. In a compare and contrast with The Sex Pistols and The Clash, he says, "The Sex Pistols are a thing in themselves: their radicalism lies in a negation that runs very, very deep. It's unlimited. There is something in the Pistols that sooner or later is going to appal anybody. And The Clash's radicalism is one of slogans, slogans communicated to Joe

Strummer and Mick Jones that made them see the world differently. The radicalism of the Gang Of Four is student radicalism, not in any put-down way – it's thoughtful, people staying up all night arguing over five pints of steery over which translation of Gramsci you ought to be using."

Marcus still marvels almost 30 years later at the intensity of the intellectual debate in GOF circles. "The talk among them was fantastic – they were so smart and well-read. They took ideas so seriously and wanted to get it right. Even if it was a song about their lack of understanding, they'd want to get it right. And it wasn't writing by committee; when Hugo or Dave would object to some way Jon or Andy were framing a line, they'd argue with him and the song would change. That's not something you got with The Clash. I'm not saying Mick Jones or Joe Strummer weren't as smart, but they plainly didn't have the same kind of education as Gang Of Four. They were told they'd never amount to anything at school, whereas Andy or Jon's teachers would have said they could be anything, a painter or a politician... They were treated very differently."

One of the qualities that most appealed to Marcus about Gang Of Four – and that marked them out from other rock revolutionaries of the time – was that they didn't trumpet their streetwise credentials. They were educated and proud of it. "What was different was that they were people like me. I'd done very few interviews and have only done a few since. But with the Gang Of Four it was like being back in graduate school: I knew people like them and they knew people like me. I didn't really interview them or ask questions, we'd just talk and there'd be arguing – what went wrong, what fucked up, which ideas didn't get across, which ideas became corrupted or confused. I just joined in with the conversation. That was different. I've not been with people like that since. There was an overwhelming earnestness about everything. Not that they were without humour or wisecracks or humiliation of people left and right – they weren't sombre, just earnest."

Burnham agrees with this assessment when he says, "People find it hard to deal with ambiguity. We were never dour. Humour was so much a part of what we did." Dave Allen neatly sums up the schizoid nature of the four GOF members when he says: "Andy was good at sniping and Jon is good at making simple lyrics about big things. He's a situationist. He's involved with the situationist community and goes to conferences. He takes it all very seriously. And that very clearly informs his lyric writing. And so on one side we could all wear shabby suits from Poland and get the beards grown and smoke a pipe, and that's one image of Gang Of Four. On the other hand, we're humans and we're here to party. I don't think that was an issue that challenged us at all. I'm sure Picasso had some fun."

However contradictory their natures, it was GOF's sheer musical power that blew audiences away. According to Burnham, "The tension was always there, and sometimes someone was late or too drunk or whatever. There were some shows that weren't so fabulous. But people were like, 'Oh, I'd better go and check them out because they're interesting, even though they're going to be a bit dour and serious and political', and they'd come away thinking, 'What the fuck was that? My God, I just had my head caved in.'"

When journalist Charles Shaar Murray joined the band in New York for an *NME* cover story in May 1980, he found them typically wrestling with the contradictions between the politics of work and leisure. "Everyone has their own indulgences," he wrote. "Burnham drinks less than the rest of the group, with Gill, the band's most rigorous theoretician, being also the band's most outrageous pisshead. In some quarters Gill is, I believe, legendary for his excesses in this direction."

Meanwhile, in between arguing vociferously about the accessibility or otherwise of certain rock-song lyrics, Jon King had this to say about GOF's twin reputations as puritanical, hard-line intellectuals and hard-core drinkers: "Our road crew when they first started working with us asked us, 'Is it all right if we drink?'

They apparently had the idea that working with Gang Of Four meant leading a fairly Spartan existence, reading *Das Kapital* in the original Sanksrit and being generally bleak and industrial." Shaar Murray concluded his article with an assessment of GOF's chances vis-à-vis Stateside success. "Watching a Gang Of Four performance, one finds it hard to believe that they cannot become a really successful group," he wrote, adding: "In 1980 it seems inconceivable that you'll hear Gang Of Four on AM radio, but in 1977 it seemed inconceivable that these US radio stations would ever be playing The Clash, and now 'Train In Vain' and 'Clampdown' are all over the radio."

If GOF were to achieve that sort of success in the US, it would be for quite different reasons than The Clash's. Compared to Joe Strummer and co, or even, say, post-punk contemporaries such as Joy Division and PiL, Gang Of Four were remarkable for their "ordinariness". "There were no stars in the band," opines Greil Marcus, "or anyone journalists could fetishise like Ian Curtis, who killed himself, or anyone charismatic or scary like John Lydon. The band weren't about personalities. They weren't performing as themselves but as versions of confused, ordinary, everyday people who somehow stumbled onto a notion of the world out of joint and not making sense. That's what they portrayed in their music and what it was about. Jon King had this laconic cool guy, vaguely studenty way of talking, and Hugo had this very clipped BBC accent, which really worked wonderfully with his skinhead appearance, but really they were four pretty ordinary people, their personal lives weren't particularly interesting, and they weren't self-destructive. You could never get a fix on these guys."

It was hearing GOF and their post-punk peers The Raincoats and Essential Logic (specifically their 12-inch single containing 'Wake Up') that encouraged Marcus to make a trip to Britain in early 1980. "I was really amazed by this music. Those three records [GOF, The Raincoats, Essential Logic] together made me think something different was happening – something remarkable. And the difference was, with each of these groups you could hear people thinking, trying to figure things out, as you listened to their songs. It was as though they were talking to themselves, and at the same time trying to speak to other people. It was tremendously exciting. That's when I decided to go to England and meet all these people and write about them."

"When Greil came to see us in England, and the live reviews starting pouring in – and I say pour in because around the world the news was insane – that's when I realised how big we were getting," says Dave Allen. Burnham, too, got a sense of how seriously GOF were being taken around the world when Marcus chose to travel to the UK to meet them. He was sent over by *Rolling Stone* in the middle of a tour. "I remember we played at a miner's strike benefit in Wakefield. It was an incredible eye-opener for him – he had to drive through the barricades, with fires and miners warming their hands and skirmishes with the cops, who were goading everyone. We had to drive past all this in the Transit van and Greil's in there with us, and with him being from Berkeley – he must have been through a lot; he'd probably seen a lot of revolutionary stuff. But to come to the north of England... And it was dark as well, so it was like a movie. It was weird even for us: this was the front line, you know? We were backstage chatting and he was asking us all about stuff and it dawned on me: 'Wow, this guy's from *Rolling Stone*.' We began to realise we were really making waves in the States."

"I travelled around England with them for days," recalls Marcus. "We stayed up late talking, but it wasn't till one night that I got this flash and understood how these songs were being communicated. And it was a breakthrough – the realisation that up till that point I hadn't understood. That's a great thrill: music you don't quite get."

Marcus denies requiring a new style of writing to deal with this startling new music. It did demand, however, "a lot of thinking and free-associating to get at what the manner of communication in Gang Of Four songs was. The voice you heard, it was very unclear where it was coming from, what figure you could connect it to. It wasn't just Andy Gill or Jon King telling you what they thought of the world. The voice is someone confused about the way the world is working, convinced that something different is going on, something utterly malevolent, and, though he's desperate to believe everything will be OK, it's a tremendously conflicted voice." The tension in GOF's music, Marcus considers, "was acted out in the cut-up structures of the music itself." The band would explain to him in very precise and thoughtful terms the way it sounded.

But he was struck by the difference between US and UK audiences, and then the contrast between audiences at the bigger and smaller shows. "The crowd were very different in England. People were dancing like crazy, they knew all the songs and were singing to themselves whether they were dancing or listening – it was a very intense crowd. The last show I saw was at the Roundhouse in early 1980, and it was godawful. Even The Mekons, to whom I would later devote much of my critical life, made no impression on me at all. And Gang Of Four were a mess, but the audience struck me – all these people milling around, wearing black leather and smoking and looking desperately ill. They had this grey pallor – I'd never seen such unhealthy looking people. And there wasn't the energy or involvement, the sense that the songs belonged to the audience, like at the smaller shows."

Marcus was particularly struck by the band's determination to make their mark and then quit on a high. "I remember when I first met them in Portsmouth, we immediately started talking and Andy said, 'This may be it, we may be dissolving the band.' I was really shocked. They said, 'Maybe we've said what we had to say in the best way we're ever going to say it, so what's the point?' That struck me as pretty remarkable, that they'd think about it that way. It was a heroic kind of thing. And in some ways maybe they should have. I don't mean that they didn't make fine music after that, but there's a way in which, when you get it right, you can leave everybody wondering, which is what happens with *Entertainment!*. Then you just disappear back into your anonymous life, but that artefact will be there for ever for people to discover, instead of having a career where the focus is on success and failure in conventional terms compared to a statement that is completely mysterious."

Greil Marcus wasn't the only legendary American music journalist that GOF met on their travels in the States. They would later encounter doyen of US gonzoid rock writing, Lester Bangs. As Dave Allen recounts, "He came backstage once and said, 'I don't fuckin' get you guys. You're shit.' We were, like, 'Lester, you're absolutely right. Have a drink, mate.' And we all got on very well. He was trying to wind us up. Or maybe he really thought we were shit." It's unlikely: GOF had the raw power and sheer hard attack of Bangs' favourite punk bands.

Burnham has vivid memories of their live carnage. "We'd kick the fucking stacks over, even my drum kit once. When we came off stage we got an absolute bollocking from our two main crew members – my brother Jol and Dave's younger brother Phil: 'You cunts, what the hell do you think you're doing? We've got to clear that up now, you wankers!' There's nothing like having a younger brother around to keep your feet on the ground. They kept us in check. But those were the good times."

Good times indeed. It was around this period that Gang Of Four were introduced to the delights of class A narcotics. "Minneapolis in 1979 was the first time we discovered coke together," recalls Burnham. "Rob came in and said, 'Oh, somebody's offered me some cocaine. Shall I buy some?' 'Yeah, why not?' And then it was like, 'That was good. Let's get some more.' And then began the steep descent. 'Let's get some more. Oh, that's quite good. Let's get some more!' I mean, fucking hell."

Not that GOF's drug-taking was either a symptom or a cause of any problems in the band. They took drugs because they enjoyed them. "It had nothing to do with problems. It was fun. That's why people take drugs: because they're fun. Now, does that mean people should take drugs in order to have fun? No. Does it mean that drugs cannot be a dreadful, destructive thing? Absolutely not. Of course they can. But why do people take drugs? *Because they're fun.* If all they did was give you a headache, make you throw up, kill you or make you mad, nobody would do them."

Did the band have to check each other for rock-star excess during this period? "Well, Andy always used to say, 'Oh, fucking Hugo, he just wants to be a rock star.' This is Andy Gill, who's perpetually in the newspapers hanging out with rock stars and getting his face about with other famous people in *Hello!* or whatever that fucking magazine is." Not that their lifestyles could ever get too extravagant – they couldn't afford it. "We couldn't afford that sort of behaviour. We were successful in every way other than monetarily."

Gill is perplexed by this accusation of rock-star cronyism, and sees it as a prime example of double standards. "We all wanted to be rock stars," he says, "but we wanted to do it in our own way, not in a clichéd way – like when Hugo got The Rolling Stones tattooed on his arm in 1979. We used to laugh at him because he used to walk on stage with a bottle of Jack Daniels swinging from his arm, and we always noticed that when he came off stage, there was exactly the same amount in it as there was before he went on! It was purely a stage prop."

However much success Gang Of Four enjoyed Stateside, the band don't feel they necessarily capitalised on it as fully as they might have done. "We never toured America like bands are supposed to," says Andy Gill. "R.E.M. were our support band for years, and suddenly they were massive, and that was because when they weren't supporting us they were doing headlining gigs as well. They did something like 320 gigs in a year. And that can pay off. I think the maximum we ever did was like four or five weeks at a time, and then we went home to bed. It's all a bit pathetic, really. We never worked particularly hard or took it as seriously as we could have done."

★　★　★

In March 1980, Gang Of Four recorded their one new release of the year: the single 'Outside The Trains Don't Run On Time', which, as part of the 'Yellow EP', also included 'He'd Send In The Army' – both tracks would later appear on the band's second album, *Solid Gold* – as well as 'It's Her Factory' from the *Entertainment!* sessions and 'Armalite Rifle' from the *Damaged Goods* EP. This four-track mini-album has been described as "like a warning shot fired across the bow of Western capitalism", but was dismissed by the *NME* as "a major disappointment".

On the opening track, Hugo Burnham and Dave Allen unleashed a minimalist yet monstrous groove that underpinned Andy Gill's jagged, funky, slash-and-burn guitar and the flat, didactic tones of Jon King. The sparest thing they ever released, 'Outside...' had a strikingly original sound. The band, however, were less than impressed with their achievements this time round, not least because of the petty arguments that occurred during the recording. "That's among my least favourite of our recordings," decides Jon King. "It was a terrible session. It had all gone tits up and we needed to argue about why, but instead the vehicle for that tension became a row about the price of a bloody Mars bar."

"We'd argue about stupid stuff constantly," laughs Andy Gill, "but Jon and Hugo were the main culprits. We spent the whole time arguing and yes, at one point, literally, over the price of a bar of chocolate: I was sat at the mixing desk with some background noise going on. I tuned in for a second to hear what the argument was about and it was about whether a Mars bar was 10p or 12p."

It was around this time that a heated debate spilled over into actual violence, during a gig in, of all places, the former Yugoslavia. Only this time it was between Allen and Gill. "Hugo and I went on for the encore," recalls King, "and wondered where Andy and Dave were. It turned out they were having a punch-up backstage about whether or not somebody had come in at the right point in one of the songs. We were purists like that. We wanted to be perfect, but you can't get perfection."

Gang Of Four got a further stab at perfection in 1980 when they began sessions for their second album, *Solid Gold*. Recorded at the famous Abbey Road studios in north London with veteran American R&B recording engineer and producer Jimmy Douglass – who had worked, most notably as far as Gang Of Four were concerned, with heavy US funk band Slave – at the helm, the album was partly the result of their experiences on the road in the States. "The thing you have to remember about America is the vast distances, which could be a bit soul-destroying," says Dave Allen, trying to summarise what it was about their American sojourn that they tried to capture on *Solid Gold*. "We had to go for very long drives, either in a bus or in vans. But I liked playing America. I liked American audiences and I think America was, itself, quite stimulating for us."

"We wrote things like 'Cheeseburger' in America," adds Gill. "I think *Solid Gold* was definitely a product of our take on America to a certain extent. I don't want to exaggerate that: other than 'Cheeseburger', there really isn't that much on the album about America. But it's clear that there are things on there that we picked up from spending quite a bit of time moseying about in America and being exposed to American culture and what was going on there; something like 'Cheeseburger', obviously, is a direct account of us being on the road in America and about how everybody else is on the road in America – it's a country that's on the road. It's also about how everybody is an immigrant. That song would have been unthinkable on *Entertainment!* because we hadn't had that kind of experience."

Gill also feels *Solid Gold* is a darker document than *Entertainment!*. Not that this reflected any darker ambience or urges within the band. "I don't think we felt it was a darker time for us as a band; just that there was a feeling that maybe politically things were getting more extreme. I have to say that a lot of the guitar stuff was new. There's feedback and sustained things that aren't just to do with the rhythms. 'Damaged Goods' is all about the guitar riff, whereas on

'Paralysed', say, it goes back and forth between the rhythm and the passages featuring sustain and feedback: the textures are combined. There are more songs like 'Paralysed' – sort of mid- to slow-tempo. There's less stuff on *Solid Gold* that's at breakneck speed.

"Rhythm has always being essential to our endeavours," he elaborates. "Like with 'He'd Send In The Army': it goes between two chords – F-sharp and G, backwards and forwards between two notes, basically. It all makes sense live: 'He'd Send In The Army' live is fucking extraordinary, with the great gaping holes in it and the stops and starts, just the drama of it. It's not really like anything else. I always liked *Solid Gold* every bit as much as, if not more than, *Entertainment!* It's funkier."

Jon King agrees, calling the album "a more danceable record. The songs have more feeling in them. I think it was a reasonable criticism that we'd been too dry before."

"Funk" was in the air when GOF began recording *Solid Gold* at the back end of 1980. Whereas *Entertainment!* was a pioneering example of punk-disco, by the time Gang Of Four came to record their second album, pop music had, in a sense, caught up with them, and bands such as A Certain Ratio, Fire Engines, Stimulin, Haircut 100, Heaven 17 and ABC (who talked in terms of a Radical Dance Faction) were beginning to incorporate elements of funk into their sound.

Ironically, or perhaps appropriately, Rob Warr bowed out of his role as band manager at the end of 1980, only to go on to work with Heaven 17 and ABC. It was ironic because those two Sheffield bands, notwithstanding their later high-gloss production, were not that far removed, ideologically, from Gang Of Four. In a way, they took GOF's ideas and, commercially, ran with them. ABC even had a song called 'Date Stamp', which talked about love as a commodity in much the same way that GOF did on *Entertainment!*

Warr's position as manager was assumed by a woman named Linda Neville. The changeover came at just the right time for Warr. "That tension between managing the band's expectations, and being their friend, got quite difficult," says Warr. "After we went to America, they were having trouble coming up with new material that was strong enough, and I just felt it was time for me to move on. I didn't want to be sitting for months on end waiting for them to come up with stuff. So I left before *Solid Gold*. We parted on extremely good terms, but I wanted to do different things and they needed a more regular manager, and we realised I didn't want to do that. I wanted greater creative input. It was my decision to leave. In the end, I wanted to be friends with them. I'm still good friends with them today."

As for Gang Of Four, all they had to do now was record an album that outstripped that classic debut and kept pace with the bands they'd so greatly influenced. "With *Entertainment!* it was that classic thing where it's the very first thing you do. You've got all the songs ready, you go in and the next thing you record them," says Dave Allen. "Then suddenly it's like, 'Guys, we're on to something!' 'But can we repeat it?' 'I dunno.' But we decided we weren't gonna rush the second album. There was no writers' block. I think the songs on *Solid Gold* speak for themselves. It was more a case of public perception – 'How do you follow *Entertainment!?*' Well, you just go and make another record. We didn't make *Entertainment!* Part II, and we were never going to. We were changing, we were growing. It might have been easier to do more of the same, but ease was never our driving force."

Nor was trying to outstrip their contemporaries, the other groups now dabbling in white funk like ABC and Stimulin. "Not really," says Burnham. "It was just like, 'This is what we like playing, this is what we like listening to.' It's where our heads were at rather than, 'OK, how do we do *Entertainment!* again?' Although having not been a commercial success, why would we have wanted to do *Entertainment!* again? But we weren't consciously avoiding it."

"Obviously people were expecting *Entertainment!* Part II, but it was more than that. And some people didn't know what to make of it," says Andy Gill, who acknowledges the pressure the band were under to move music on a second time. "I think you are kind of aware that people want something pretty special out of you, but I guess you can't keep reinventing the wheel." There was, however, no commercial pressure on them to right the wrongs of the *Top Of The Pops*/"rubbers" fiasco. "I quite admired Heaven 17's transformation from being a band influenced by Gang Of Four into a big, brash and shiny pop group who adopted some of the best aspects of American funk and soul; and ABC did something similar, but in a less clever way, I think. But I don't think there's anything about *Solid Gold* that is a more commercial version of *Entertainment!* It's not the way I see it anyway. The sound was maybe not quite as brittle, but that's it." At the same time, Gill agrees GOF were never about making deliberately awkward, "difficult" music. "There was a lot of criticism when we signed to EMI: 'You should be on Rough Trade', that sort of thing. And it was like, you're missing the point. That's not what we're about. We're not trying to be difficult and hard-to-understand. We're not trying to be avant garde. I mean, there might be some pretty out-there things that we're doing, but we want our records in the charts or whatever. To us, that's half the point."

Solid Gold is, as Greil Marcus said of the musicians themselves, quite hard to get a fix on, being neither a left-field experiment nor a simple bid for commercial acceptance. One of the more extreme assessments of GOF's second album didn't appear till well after the event. In Garry Mulholland's superb 2006 book, *Fear Of Music: The 261 Greatest Albums Since Punk And Disco*, the author makes quite bold, controversial claims for the record. "[*Solid Gold* is] the best completely tuneless record ever made," he writes. "The Gang Of Four, hung up on booze, drugs, deep funk and the imminent collapse of the human soul under the onslaught of Eighties free market economics, bury melody under the clammy silt of Afro-funk rhythm that even the inventor of the beat-is-the-tune idea, James Brown, might consider a tad extreme. Considered a career-suicide album by some, the absolute essence of the band by others,

Solid Gold is unflinching in its despair, relentless in its rhythms, bleakly appropriate in its fit of medium to message, and horrifyingly right about everything."

"That's a brilliant review," Gill responds to the above remarks, "but I'd never thought it to be any of those things. I think we were conscious of the fact that we were in a difficult position, but we certainly weren't suicidal; there was no volition in that area. We were just continuing down the rather difficult path that we'd set ourselves. There was no sense of sabotage." He does concede, however, that GOF resisted any attempts to "poppify" their sound. "Me and Jon can often sit down and write great pop songs with a little bridge and lovely transitions from the verse to the chorus; we can finely craft a pop song," he admits. "But what's the point of doing that – to make money? I think you fall flat on your arse if you do that. We sort of did it with 'I Love A Man In Uniform', but people really have got their detectors out for, 'They're not being true to themselves,' you know? It's tricky. You have a fan base, and people that are into you expect certain things."

Gill confirms that Jimmy Douglass was invited to produce *Solid Gold* because of his production for numerous American funk acts. He remembers the veteran producer coming to see the band play for the first time and, as they ran through six or seven potential demos of songs for *Solid Gold*, being simultaneously amazed and bemused. "I said, 'What do you think?' And he said, 'You all sound so English.' I was quite pleased. To him, we were talking in a foreign language. And he was like, 'What the fuck is this?' But he was quite thrilled by it. He even wrote a two-page article for *Producer* magazine about working on *Solid Gold*, and he was massively complimentary. He said that he thought he knew what production was about until he worked on *Solid Gold*. He said he found what Jon and I were doing was fascinating and he learned so much from it. It was quite a brave thing to write, because he was a massively successful, well-known producer, and he was basically saying, 'I had all my ideas turned upside down by Gang Of Four.'"

For Hugo Burnham, working with Douglass was a joy compared with his experiences two years earlier. "It was quite tense," he says of the *Entertainment!* sessions. "I'm not complaining, I'm just making an observation, but there was a lot of pressure on us. There was a definite tension. We were four very talented people – four aggressively talented people – but by the time me and Dave finished our takes and went up to the control room, there was no space for us. That's why you don't see mine or Dave's name on the production credits. God bless that record, it was extraordinary. But it wasn't enjoyable for me. *Solid Gold* was much more enjoyable because I didn't feel the same pressure, and we had a co-producer who managed us better. It was a lot more fun because Jimmy Douglass took a little bit of the strain – that thing of being less like a team and more like Jon and Andrew running things. I think having a real producer took away the thing of, 'Fucking hell, we're being excluded and those two are taking over.' It didn't feel quite that desperate. Look, realistically, any group has to have some sort of a leader. But a good leader also has a responsibility not to be solipsistic about everything, and not to just bully things through. That was part of the pressure on Dave."

The band were, considers Burnham, more of a "gang of four" on the second album than the first. "Yeah, in some ways. I look back on recording *Solid Gold* with fonder memories. It wasn't as difficult for me. I felt a lot more confident by that time in the recording process. Because if Jimmy said, 'Oh, you didn't get that quite right,' you know, he was telling me I didn't get it quite right, whereas whenever Andrew said I didn't do something quite right, there was always an unpleasant tone to it. But the second album was great fun to make; it was a really good record, but again it went nowhere commercially."

Beyond the band politics, Burnham doesn't believe there was additional pressure on them to match that debut album, mainly because it hadn't sold as well as many had anticipated. "I think if it had sold a lot and been commercially successful we would have felt more pressure. But I certainly remember enjoying recording *Solid Gold* more than *Entertainment!* because it was less the front row versus the back row, as it were. It was more of a band effort, because the producer levelled the playing field. Jon, Andrew and I were very much involved, sitting around the desk all day. It was a much easier record to make. I didn't feel nearly so pressured performance-wise in the studio, and I thought we had some great songs. I loved the slightly heavier, funkier direction. And being at Abbey Road was a blast."

So is *Solid Gold* "the best completely tuneless record ever made"? Burnham believes that's more a case of, "God, I'm writing about the Gang Of Four. I'd better bring my game on, and I'd better get a thesaurus right next to me." As for the notion of "career suicide", he says, "Well, the album didn't sell very well, but that was all right. We weren't doing it for that, although obviously we were disappointed not to sell a lot because selling a lot is really about getting through to people: it means people are loving it. And I think there was some mystification about how we'd sell out tours everywhere we went and people raved about us to our faces at shows, but we couldn't get arrested sales-wise. But I don't feel there was any sense in which we were doing anything negative on *Solid Gold*. I love that record. I enjoyed recording it more, it was a much nicer atmosphere. We hadn't been dropped by EMI even though *Entertainment!* hadn't done very well, we still felt strongly about what we were doing, the songs were really good and I loved playing them. We were strong."

Burnham fondly recalls the sessions in Abbey Road's Studio 2, the room used by The Beatles for almost all of their recordings, although he recognised that Douglass "found us strange to work with, because we were quite aggressive about what we wanted, both as a group and individually. He expected us to just play the parts and let him get on with it, and anyone who thought that about Gang Of Four was sorely mistaken. I think he learned quite a lot from us, actually, as well." He cites 'What We All Want' as "perennially one of my favourite songs of all time. Playing it live was always like a steam shovel. I think Jimmy recognised that as being the closest to the things he'd worked on before: big, steamy and funky. It's a fantastic song. 'Outside The Trains Don't Run On Time' was so jerky and weird that I loved it: great polyrhythmic stuff, you know, going back to my Charlie Watts roots."

Finally, Burnham believes the band, now somewhat older and more experienced, could afford to relax a little on *Solid Gold*. "There was less pressure on us than there was with *Entertainment!.*. Then, we'd just got this big deal after we'd chased all the labels, and it was almost like, 'Can they, will they?' I remember being on the front cover of *Sounds* with Joe Jackson for a Bands To Watch feature in 1979. There was a lot of pressure, internally as well, but I think we just relaxed into it a bit more by the time we got to record *Solid Gold*."

Solid Gold may not have been as shattering and original as its predecessor, and yet in 'Paralysed', 'Why Theory?', 'If I Could Keep It For Myself', 'He'd Send In The Army' and the quaking 'What We All Want', it contained many startling examples of GOF's harsh, angular rock-funk, while also offering, as one American critic put it, "a valuable psycho-social record of the swing to the New Right that occurred in both Britain and the US at the turn of the decade." Reviews in the UK press were less ecstatic than for the debut album – although Adam Sweeting of *Melody Maker* felt that "with *Solid Gold*, Gang Of Four have deliberately steered away from the abrasive polemics of their earlier material. They've gone instead for more of a cohesive feel" – while in America they chose this moment to embrace the group they were calling "the best politically motivated dance band in rock'n'roll." From 1981 onwards they'd play the majority of their remaining concerts there. Tom Carson in the *Village Voice* concluded that, "live, this young English band comes up with rock'n'roll urgency to match their intellectual commitment." In a four-star *Rolling Stone* review, Milo Miles wrote: "Despite the heavy irony of its title, *Solid Gold* does have a pre-sold audience: rock fans who consider themselves safely outside the mainstream and revel in music that faces up to what they assume are unpopular truths. The clincher comes with 'Why Theory?', which revolves around a two-note melodica riff that echoes the childlike insistence in King's voice. A thoroughly abstract song-as-thesis, the song contains the vaguely Marxist kernel of the Gang Of Four's insight: humanity is the unconscious product of its social net ('We've all got opinions/Where do they come from?/Each day seems like a natural fact')." The reviewer concluded that, despite a certain tendency towards "a leaden obviousness" musically and lyrically ("it skewers too many standard villains, such as McDonald's in 'Cheeseburger', or resurgent fascists in 'Outside The Trains Don't Run On Time'), Gang Of Four seemed to have found a higher calling for rock'n'roll: "didactics you can dance to."

So all was good in Gang Of Four land. Or so it seemed. Unfortunately, during another US tour of duty, just after the release of *Solid Gold* in March 1981, one of the band decided they'd had enough, and quit.

CHAPTER 6

SONG OF THE FREE

"I think my leaving was quite traumatic for the other three. Because I broke that bond. But perhaps we just didn't buy into the romanticism of the Last Gang In Town." – Dave Allen

Already by the start of 1981, only four years after they formed and just over two since they released their debut EP, Gang Of Four's days as a gang of four were numbered. Dave Allen's swansong as a member of GOF was the *Another Day/Another Dollar* EP comprising 'Capital (It Fails Us Now)', 'History's Bunk!', live versions of 'Cheeseburger' and 'What We All Want', and the awesome death disco of lead-off track, 'To Hell With Poverty.'

But as far as Jon King was concerned, the writing was on the wall when the sessions began for the EP at London's Townhouse studios with producer Nick Launay, then only in his early twenties but with recordings by the likes of The Jam, XTC, PiL, Killing Joke and The Birthday Party already under his belt. "We'd argue about what a chord was – a chord was two notes at the same time," says the singer, although he was pleased with the finished product. "I actually wrote 'To Hell With Poverty', which didn't have any chords in it. No chords, no verse, no bridge, no chorus. It was a brilliant song. But it was written because we were being programmatical: 'We're not going to have any chords.' And then, weirdly, we got Dave to write this amazing hard-core funk bottom end to it – it's still played as a dance record to this day."

Although this was to be their final recording session in their original incarnation, Hugo Burnham has fond memories of working on 'To Hell With Poverty'. "I still think, to this day, that was the best recording we ever did," he considers. "It's certainly the truest in sound and fury to the way we played live. That song captured it best. And Nick Launay was the best producer we ever had. He was great, even if we came to him too late. Dave left after that and the mood changed… But the three days in the Townhouse were terrific. It was great fun."

Burnham, with his loathing of rehearsing and playing in dark rooms and dimly lit studios, remembers the studio being very bright, with lots of windows. It helped that 'To Hell…' was, in his words, "just a fucking fantastic song" that came fairly quickly to them; that, for once, the band hadn't "agonised" over a piece of music. It was a particularly enjoyable session for Burnham and Allen because it was the rhythm section who came up with the B-side, 'Capital (It Fails Us Now)', that excoriating examination of the lie-dream of the capitalist ethos with the pounding bass-drum beat and piledriving bass. "I approached it in, I won't say a mechanical way, but it was fairly metronomic but interesting," Burnham explains his dub-spacious technique on the track. "Not fiddly-interesting. I hate fiddly drummers. It's just like, go back to Simon Kirke [drummer with early-Seventies rockers Free] – fucking bang, wallop, but not just a cacophony. You leave spaces, gaps. Whether me as a drummer, Andy as a guitar player or Dave as a bass player, we all understood that. It was interesting. It created tension." His drumming style, he says, could be described as "funk that's not funk", created by "leaving a couple of things out". No rolls around the drum kit for Burnham ("It wasn't my thing"). "Listen to 'Why Theory?' or 'Outside The Trains Don't Run On Time'," he suggests. "That really encapsulates my style of drumming."

Nick Launay was the son of bohemian parents (his father was noted French author Andre Launay) who had been living in southern Spain since he was eight but had just moved back to London at the time. Despite having worked with some of the biggest names in alternative rock, from The Slits to Supergrass, INXS to Yeah Yeah Yeahs, he fondly recalls the events of 1981, even when the going got tumultuous. "I'd just done PiL's *Flowers Of Romance* and an EP with The Birthday Party called 'Release The Bats'; then I produced Killing Joke, so I was used to stroppy post-punkers," he laughs. "I was a stroppy post-punker! Gang Of Four were one of my favourite bands so I was thrilled to be working with them. It was a lovely thing to have done. They were a similar age, and had the same influences as me, so we went in and made a racket; the right kind of racket." Launay had been working at the Townhouse as a tape operator/assistant before graduating to production. His first credit was on PiL's 'Flowers Of Romance', his second *what's THIS for...!* by Killing Joke, his third 'Release The Bats' by Nick Cave's crew. 'To Hell With Poverty' was his fourth production job. "The band contacted me," he recalls. "I was about 21 years old and had only really just started, but I'd already worked with PiL on their 'Flowers Of Romance' single and got on really well with John [Lydon], and that led to doing the album [also called *Flowers Of Romance*]. I guess because of the attention I was receiving, a lot of bands started getting in touch with me."

Gang Of Four were live wires in the studio, even given the company Launay had been keeping. "It was fantastic," says the producer. "They were quite political and there were certainly a lot of discussions, as well as a fair amount of arguing. But it was all very constructive. I got the impression that that was just the way they were. There were some very strong-headed people in that band. Their arguing about artistic things led to the records they made, which wasn't a problem. I hate it when bands bring outside bullshit into the studio, but their arguing was to do with the passionate feelings they had about the way music should sound and how it should be presented; musical things and lyrical things. It led to some pretty heavy discussions." Could he tell they were on their last legs as the original four-piece? "Not at all," he says. "I wouldn't have guessed I'd do the last EP of the original members. But I do remember a lot of raised voices in the studio. I didn't think anyone was genuinely cross, though – it was just normal passionate discussions. I was so young and obsessed; I wasn't old enough to know about relationships. I just wanted to record great music, and I was in heaven. The arguments were just in the background and it was none of my business. Sure, Andy Gill is a very opinionated man and he could be hot-headed and fly off the handle, but then Johnny Rotten and Nick Cave were quite opinionated, so that was normal for me. Besides, I'd rather that than someone wishy-washy who sounds like someone else."

Launay says the project came together quite easily, and that they spent two days in total recording the EP. The producer had particular sounds in mind for the tracks. "My influences were the same as theirs, so not a lot needed to be said. I love heavy, angry sounds and to make rebellious music is, for me, a natural thing. The music I'd been making up to that point was in the same ballpark. 'To Hell…' and 'Capital (It Fails Us Now)' fit in well with that." He was impressed by the band as a whole, as well as by the individual players. "Andy Gill is the absolute king of feedback," he says, still impressed by Gill's special home-made gold Fender Stratocaster guitar. "No one gets feedback like Andy Gill, not even Hendrix. When it comes to getting feedback to sing – listen to the beginning of 'To Hell With Poverty' and you know something amazing will follow. The fact that it's a disco beat is the shocker. It starts off anarchistic, abrasive and in-yer-face and then it turns into disco, and yet the feedback carries on. He's one of the most important guitar players ever and has influenced every interesting guitar player since. He does feedback and rhythm – he's a great rhythm guitarist. He obviously listens to a lot of funk players, but he adds that distorted sound.

"Then, of course, there's Dave Allen – his bass-playing is an amazing part of that sound. On both songs I did with them, he had two bass parts and on 'Capital...' he plays three different parts, all with different sounds. What a player! So you had a great combination of a unique-sounding guitar player who uses feedback to create melody, a bassist with the most driven, anarchistic rock-bass sound but who plays funk bass, plus a drummer to hold it all together who plays very simple yet contagious and danceable beats. And finally you had Jon King, who was basically a rock politician, on vocals. The only other bands in the same area of dance music were PiL although they leaned more toward dub reggae, and Killing Joke, but they were much heavier, almost metal, all about aggression and evil. Gang Of Four weren't evil, just political."

'To Hell With Poverty' was GOF's plain grooviest song to date. "It was confrontational disco with a message," says Launay. "Without them, the idea of a white indie band playing funk would be inconceivable. They made disco cool. This certainly wasn't *Saturday Night Fever.*" But he isn't sure if there was any intention for it to be a hit. "It wasn't discussed but deep down, behind all the usual 'we-just-want-to-do-it-for-ourselves', there's always the hope that some miracle will happen where a left-of-centre record might get through to more people than their current audience. But it's not something you manipulate. As soon as you make records trying to follow trends you're fucked. This has been my experience time and time again. If you work with truly gifted people who have a vision and try to take them down the road to sell to lots of people, you'll lose what you've already got – what makes them original and different."

Today, almost three decades on, Launay still rates the EP as one of the best things he's ever worked on. In fact, when pushed to pick his own personal top five or six tracks with his name on, he ranks both 'To Hell...' and 'Capital (It Fails Us Now)' in his personal pantheon alongside 'Four Enclosed Walls' by PiL, 'Down

Boy' by Yeah Yeah Yeahs, 'No Pussy Blues' by Grinderman and 'Release The Bats' by The Birthday Party. He also considers *Entertainment!* to be one of the most important records ever made – "Up there," he says, "with Bowie's '*Heroes*', The Stooges' *Raw Power*, The Sex Pistols' *Never Mind The Bollocks* and Talking Heads' *Remain In Light*."

He believes that, notwithstanding Gang Of Four's peers such as A Certain Ratio and The Pop Group, GOF were in a class of their own when it came to pioneering a white funk sound. "Gang Of Four did it most successfully," he says. "Pretty much all the American bands I work with these days love the Gang Of Four and talk about them. They're very current. I'm working with Yeah Yeah Yeahs, and there's definitely a hats-off to the Gang Of Four from them. Most of the bands in the last few years who play dance music with loud beats and loud hi-hats are influenced by them."

In terms of impact and underground cult appeal, Launay considers Gang Of Four to be the post-punk equivalent of The Velvet Underground. "They were the only white band who came before GOF that made danceable music that was cool," he says, "even though I don't think they went out of their way to make dance music. The Chili Peppers came from a very sexual place, and they were about showing off their bodies because they were healthy, whereas Gang Of Four were skinny white guys who were about wearing suits and looking smart in a fucked-up way. But ultimately the Chilis' music is dance music, and there's a certain amount of politics in their early music, so there's a mutual admiration there. Nirvana were big fans, too, and Modest Mouse have moments of Gang Of Four-dom. And these bands sell a lot of records!"

Launay believes that, had Dave Allen stayed with the band, he might have been called upon to produce their third album, but, he says, "I think they were so intrigued by the possibility of making a record that actually sold that they and their record company wanted to try someone a bit more commercial, so they went with a more commercially successful producer." Besides, he adds, "Things changed when Dave Allen left." Nevertheless, having worked with Allen again when he produced a bizarre avant-garde version of 'Le Freak' by Chic when the bassist was in a band called Restaurant For Dogs with Barry Andrews of XTC, Launay insists he'd love to collaborate with the original four again, were they to iron out their differences. "It was a pleasure," he says, "to work with them."

★ ★ ★

Around this time, however, life in the Gang Of Four wasn't actually much of a pleasure for Dave Allen. Andy Gill remembers sharing a hotel room with him one night while the band were on the road in the States following the release of *Solid Gold*, and the bassist didn't seem happy. "He just went quieter and quieter and quieter," recalls Gill, "until I said, 'Are you all right? You look kind of depressed.' And to this day I don't think he's ever quite explained what it was that was wrong."

In fact, in an interview with the author, Allen does, for the first time ever, explain why it was he was so unhappy and what it was that made him decide to leave the group. "My leaving Gang Of Four was a consistent struggle with my personality," he reveals. "There were expectations that put me under pressure and manifested themselves with me doing tons of drugs. I tried to bury all my feelings. The idea was sort of, if I'm out of my brains all day it might stop the noise in my head, you know?

"My personality is strong, and meeting people is easy for me," he continues, "but at the same time I was trying to reconcile that with the big ideas that Jon and Andy had for Gang Of Four – they grasped those notions about where the band was going. And it took me a few years to grasp them myself."

Allen puts his unhappiness in the band down to feelings of inadequacy, brought on by what he calls Gill and King's "superior education". Eventually, through self-education, he caught up with his former band-mates, but it was too late for him to ever feel fully integrated into GOF. He was capable of grasping the concepts explored by Gill and King in the band's music but he just didn't have the confidence to realise it. "During the band years, I was conflicted," he says. "I fully understood everything but I couldn't reconcile it in myself as a working-class kid – some of the stuff that was being discussed with people like Greil Marcus. I had my own thoughts about it, but we were a united force so I buried a lot of it. I kept quiet."

In a way, Allen felt that GOF's songs were about things he, as a working-class lad, had actually experienced but was unable to articulate. "I don't want to be on the therapist's couch and I don't want to undermine anything Jon and Andy wrote – anything they said was accurate and I think the points of view they expressed were exceptionally precise – but how they got to that point was a puzzle for me." Allen would feel particularly self-conscious during interviews with the music press, in which journalists tended to explore the meaning of GOF songs in complex language. "I'd be with all these journalists, only 21 or 22 years old... I wonder now if I was a bit slower in my development. I was challenging myself about it and making myself feel a bit guilty about it. I'd spend two full days in the Warner Brothers office in New York at the beginning of a tour, doing 10 interviews a day with some very learned people like Nick Kent, Charles Shaar Murray and Paul Morley... These were very bright people, and they'd be discussing the theory of everything. Let's just say the little guy from Kendal was at times confused. I'm not ashamed of that, but at the time I might have been. I felt guilty. I was supposed to be this member of Gang Of Four, these big thinkers, but at that time I wasn't that big a thinker. I am now – I'm very comfortable in my skin now, and have been for many years. But back then I was struggling – the working-class kid brought up to not expect anything, whose parents had no money, so that pair of jeans has to last you till they're completely falling off your backside... That's what probably made me want to get out. You know, like, 'I'm kinda done with this prison.'"

Feeling out of place, Allen sought refuge in drugs. "I would say very safely and knowledgeably that I was totally addicted to cocaine," he admits. His addiction began on tour in America in 1979, and continued until his departure, also while on tour in the States, in early 1981. He wasn't the only one in the GOF camp doing drugs; he just did more of them, more often. "It's hard to deny that that was the culture. I liked playing and I liked going out after the shows and I liked running after the girls, and that meant staying up all night – what better way to stay up all night than to do a lot of charlie, eh? Then, the next day, you get horribly interrupted sleep. You're on a tour bus and you don't realise that you're actually becoming mentally and physically exhausted. You begin to not make rational decisions. And so you ask the tour manager for more [drugs] for the night's show, otherwise you won't feel up to it. And so the cycle begins. You can't get off that friggin' horse, you know? It's very tough. Couple that with a lot of anxieties about all sorts and you're a psychiatrist's dream."

Before he knew it, what began as "casual drug use" became full-scale addiction. "It's what you're supposed to do," he explains. "We'd go to Amsterdam and I'd meet this beautiful woman I used to date, and she was totally into casual use of cocaine before going to a gig. If we were there for a few days it would be a fucking drug binge. 'Let's get loads of that stuff, ha ha ha! And while we're at it, we'll get a load of vodka, some wine and beer and we don't have to go out!' And we didn't. We'd stay in for three days. I'd come back to London like a zombie."

Allen believes GOF's vague air of puritanical abstention, however illusory, "may have added to my issues." Following therapy, Allen managed to wean himself off drugs, but he still needed help to stay off them. Among the people who helped him was rock politico Tom Robinson. "He was really good," says Allen. "He got me a good therapist in London, and I had some good sessions. He was digging around in my whole background. He felt there was something there – I wasn't that old, right? But he felt there was something in my recent past. He was good at opening my mind to the ball and chain that was my upbringing. And once I got beyond that hurdle, once I felt good about talking about it, it all evaporated. Once I started telling people that the thing about, 'Poor old Dave who left the Gang Of Four because he was all fucked-up on drugs' had a bit of a backstory… That was just the public face of my inner turmoil."

Broadly speaking, the turmoil sprang from his insecurity about lacking an education that was up to being one of the Gang Of Four. "That's a good, simple way of putting it," he agrees. "I felt less than adequate. Most people get into that downward spiral when they feel less than adequate. And I feel that for such a social animal as I am, that was a blow to my confidence. You gravitate to people that are in your own social class and your educational level to make you feel good about yourself. I don't hang out with professors who talk to me about stuff I don't know about. And I think that there was a bit of that with the band – I knew where we were at musically and lyrically, but there was another layer: the philosophical ideas, like Marxism – that's where it got to be a very grey area for me."

Allen's feelings of alienation were exacerbated by an additional sense of isolation from the Gill-King axis. "Jon and Andrew grew up together, went to school together, and ended up at the same college together, so they always had that tied-at-the-hip relationship where they could finish each other's sentences," he says. "They were both incredibly confident people with some good ideas and they learned quickly about political systems and their manifestations. And so they would talk long into the night with a bottle of wine."

He now believes that taking refuge in narcotics, alcohol and casual sex was a mistake, and that without them he "may have just grown up with the guys and learned something every day. I might have felt like, 'This is fabulous. This is better than going to college.'"

But, he adds, he wants to play down the druggy and sexual excess. "It was just the usual – you're in a band so you find girls. Somebody will come along and there are usually drugs involved. But I take the blame for the drug thing. Really, it was nothing to do with the band, and nothing to do with circumstances. I just got addicted to something I shouldn't have got addicted to. Maybe I would have just become an alcoholic otherwise, I don't know. It's like, well, something was going to happen."

Something did: he left the band during the US tour following the release of *Solid Gold*. As Allen puts it, "I was becoming a fuck-up and I wanted to fix it. I had to leave for my own good. Credit to the other three for ploughing on." Today, Allen believes his departure to have been "quite traumatic for the other three. Because I broke that bond. But perhaps we just didn't buy into the romanticism of the Last Gang In Town."

Andy Gill sensed that Allen "felt out of his depth, and that led him to do the things that he did. He felt he wasn't quite up to the rigorous intellectual whatever, all the things around Gang Of Four. Almost as though he felt outside of things that he was meant to be involved in. And I think that got to him. He should have talked about it. But he didn't; he just went very, very silent. I kept asking him what was up because I really, really liked him. When we were touring he was a great guy; really funny and charming. But you often can't see things like that – 'Oh, perhaps Dave is intimidated by me being too clever.'"

For Gill, the problems started becoming apparent during the recording of *Solid Gold*. When they were making *Entertainment!* they were able to maintain the illusion of democracy, even if it was just that – an illusion. "Yes, all four of us argued about decision-making, whether we should have a cup of tea or whether we should have a pint of beer," says Gill, "but the generation of ideas for the songs came from me and Jon. You know: 'This is the pattern I'd like you to play', all that. But we would do interviews like we were four equal partners. There's always the tension between the individual and the unit. It's never going to be smooth sailing every day, is it? And there's always going to be politics where you say, 'Hold on a minute, if I've done all the work on this, and you've been down the pub, why…' You know, those questions get raised.

"The crack started to gape open during *Solid Gold* really," he continues. "That's when Dave started complaining about the songwriting process. So me and Jon said to him, 'Well, why don't you come up with more ideas, then? Why don't you bring something to us?' And he said, 'OK, I will, if we get individual credits.' That's where the idea for individually crediting different people for their contributions began. That's why on *Solid Gold* you start seeing, 'Written by Gill,' or 'Written by Gill-King.' Which was, ironically, an idea initially refused by Dave."

Prior to Allen announcing that he was quitting, recalls Gill, there had been an incident in Liverpool where the bassist hadn't turned up to a gig – "Which did," he says, "slightly raise alarm bells." That night, they talked about postponing the show but believed it to be "an aberration", so they soldiered on. He can't remember the exact American date Allen left on, but he does recall what he said: "Basically, he said, 'I don't want to continue. I want to go home.' So he just upped and left. I remember handing him his passport and a bunch of money and saying, 'Well, I hope you feel all right.' We were somewhere in the middle of America. We had to cancel several shows. We thought, 'OK, well, that's it. We'd better go back to England.'"

Hugo Burnham doesn't remember the Allen-goes-missing-in-Liverpool incident – actually, he believes it was Manchester, and that it was Andy Gill who went AWOL – but he does say, "It wouldn't surprise me." Gill is emphatic about this accusation. "Hugo's a fucking idiot for saying that. I know it was Liverpool, and that it was Dave who went missing, because me and Jon had to stand on stage at [club] Eric's and explain to the audience that Dave had been hurt in a traffic accident and that we wouldn't be playing. We were shitting ourselves because the crowd were so

Gang Of Four get to the roof of the matter. (**URBANIMAGE.TV/ADRIAN BOOT**)

Live at Virgin Megastore, London, 1980. To cut a long story short, they invented New Romantic as well…
(RAFAEL MACIA/REDFERNS)

Live in New York, 1980. US audiences took even more readily to GoF's angular,
visceral racket than their British counterparts. **(EBET ROBERTS/REDFERNS)**

In the States in 1980, the band find the solution to that old leisure/pleasure conundrum.
(COURTESY OF HUGO BURNHAM)

Dave Allen by Hugo Burnham, 1980.
(HUGO BURNHAM)

GoF examine dialectical materialism in the British Film industry merely by standing outside Pinewood Studios in 1981. **(ALASTAIR INDGE/RETNA)**

Punk-funk's crucial three stagefront at the Lyceum, London, June 7, 1981. (**DAVID CORIO/REDFERNS**)

In the EMI office, Manchester Square, London, 1981. Duran who? (**BRIAN RASIC/REX FEATURES**)

A naked Flea from the Red Hot Chili Peppers stage rushes Jon in LA, 1981, right after Dave quit the band.
(COURTESY OF HUGO BURNHAM)

Welcome to Woman Town. With Sara Lee (front) and Eddie Reader, 1982. **(LFI)**

Hugo and Sara backstage at a festival with Sting, in 1982. **(COURTESY OF HUGO BURNHAM)**

Onstage at a US festival, 1982, photo taken by Sara Lee. "That was a happy time for us." **(SARA LEE)**

Steve Goulding, GoF drum for hire after Hugo's departure. **(COURTESY OF ANDY GILL)**

Andy, Sara and Jon in London, circa *Hard*. **(FIN COSTELLO/REDFERNS)**

Taken from the 1995 video for 'Tattoo'. Jon used ether to remove the paint – the solvent, not the song. **(JUSTIN THOMAS)**

At the Mojo awards in London, June 16, 2005. "We knew we could do it because we still had all our own hair!" (LFI)

Andy onstage at a radio contest in Atlanta, GA, October 7, 2005. "When it comes to feedback, he's up there with Hendrix." (ROBB D COHEN/RETNA)

The tattooed bass supremo at the Wireless Festival, Hyde Park, June 25, 2006. (BRIAN RASIC/REX FEATURES)

The last ever publicity shot of the Fab Four of feedback funk, before Hugo and Dave's departure.

fucking angry. We nearly got beaten up by the bouncers. It was pretty heavy."

As far as Burnham recalls, Allen finally called it quits not in America but in Canada. "I think it all came to a head in Toronto," says the drummer, "because our management at the time – who spent more time doing sulphate and basically not doing their job – hadn't got any visas for our crew, so they were stopped on the way from Toronto back to the States and got sent home. It was my brother Jolyan, Dave's brother Phil, Kevin Harvey, our sound man, and our lighting guy, Ray Watouski, who was a ray of light. Actually, Ray was an American citizen so they let him straight in, and Kevin Harvey snuck his way back in, but Jolyan and Phil, that was the last we ever saw of them, so it was all a bit sad."

Burnham is aware of the band's penchant for narcotics – after all, he was immersed himself – but he acknowledges that Allen was more heavily involved than the others. "There was lots of fucking cocaine. But Dave cracked first. I think that's the best way to put it. He was having a miserable time: we had to give him coke to get on stage, and he'd sit in a corner under a towel rocking back and forth. The worst thing was we weren't very kind to him during all this. We weren't really aware that he was actually in real trouble."

Burnham understands that the drugs were a symptom, not the cause, of the problem. It was Allen's feelings of inadequacy that were the crux of the matter. "Andrew and Jon are not exactly intellectual bullies, but they were very forceful about their ideas. I understood it more, and I think Dave not really having had a good solid public school education and not having been to university found it hard keeping up. It was intimidating waffle, a lot of it. I mean, Jon is a very intelligent, well-read man, and continues to be to this day. Andrew is just this artistic, intellectual bully.

"I remember him saying, 'I can't do it any more, I'm going home.' It was during this meeting in a room in the Iroquois Hotel in New York. It was our tour manager and the four of us, and he [Allen] just left. I remember Jon and Andrew being livid. And I followed him out of the room and gave him a big hug. I said, 'Don't worry about it, man. Go home and be safe.'"

Burnham didn't think Allen's departure signalled the end of the band, but he worried that the tour was now in jeopardy. His, Gill and King's response was immediate, and decisive. "We went out," says Burnham, "and got very drunk and high." It was Steve Baker from Warner Brothers, GOF's A&R man on America's East Coast, who really snapped into action. "He came with us [for a drink] and said, 'Fuck it, let's get another bassist.'"

The band did, indeed, now urgently require a new bassist, because they had a series of sold-out shows on the West Coast to play and only two-and-a-half days in New York to turn the crisis back into a drama. Calls went out to many people. It was Baker who managed to offer Gill, King and Burnham a ray of hope. "He said, 'Don't let this stop you in your tracks. Get somebody else in,'" says Gill. Burnham remembers Bill Laswell being approached as replacement for Allen and him agreeing, only for the innovative funk bassist's manager to change his mind on his client's behalf within hours. Fortunately, with less than a day before GOF's first show without Allen, in Seattle, renowned bass supremo Busta "Cherry" Jones, who had played on, among many things, David Byrne and Brian Eno's seminal sample-fest *My Life In The Bush Of Ghosts*, was found.

"Over the space of about 12 or 14 hours," recalls Gill, "he figured out how to play all the songs. It was amazing." It was a memorable show, all told. It was sold out, for starters. And, as far as Gill remembers it, man-mountain Tad Doyle, later of legendary local grungesters Tad, was in the audience. So too was a 16-year-old kid named Kurt Cobain – "Or at least, that's what I'm told by the Seattle people. It was just real high energy, and everything gelled."

It felt like a rebirth of sorts. "If you imagine how down we were, what with Dave going off and everything… It was like, 'What do we do now?' Suddenly we were thrown this lifeline – a very effective lifeline."

Inevitably there was some disappointment that GOF hadn't managed to retain the ideological purity of the original venture – the four-piece – featuring the John, Paul, George and Ringo of post-punk funk. "I was disappointed and sad about it," admits Gill. "When one of the original members goes, it sort of changes things a bit, doesn't it? But you adapt to your circumstances. What can we do if someone says, 'I'm going, I'm quitting'? It was just good that we had the option to go on."

At this point, nobody knew whether the late, great Jones was to be a permanent replacement for Allen. Gill just remembers that, apart from being a superb bassist, "he was a bit fond of coke". Burnham's view is that Gill and King assumed it would be too late for Jones to learn the necessary bass parts in time. "Jon and Andy said, 'It's too late. Nobody can learn it in this time.' Steve [Baker] and I were more, 'Let's give it a crack.' So we did, and he came in with a little Walkman in one hand, and he was literally listening to the songs and playing them with the other hand. Andy was like, 'If he doesn't get it the first time, fuck it, I'm going home.' I said, 'Fucking hell, Andrew, come on. Let's be positive.' You know, the same old dynamic. But he [Jones] was great. And he lifted us enormously. It was all quite exciting – he was very hip and groovy; he was the dude."

The Seattle gig was at a venue called The Show Box, where the band Three Swimmers was the support act. GOF managed to negotiate their way through the first song without any difficulties. "It was like, 'OK, we can do this,'" says Burnham. By the third song, King and Gill were careening into each other with their usual gusto and verve. "It was like, 'We're back,'" says Burnham, who remembers Jones looking at him incredulously as Gill and King did their party piece. "He looks at them doing this, banging into each other, and he turns around to me and says, 'What the fuck?' And I said, 'Go, go!', like this. So he just puts his head down and charges right at them.

"Busta was a lovely guy," he adds. "He really lived life to the fullest. I hate that expression, but he brought this enthusiasm and an ability to say, 'Fuck it, I can do it.' He brought us back. But he was like a shooting star that came into our firmament and lit up the night sky, and then was gone."

There is some confusion about what happened next: some believe The Rolling Stones tried to coax Jones into their fold in the event of Bill Wyman's rumoured departure, others that he just wanted to move on. But all agree that the temporary bassist was too fond of class As to be a permanent replacement, even for Gang Of Four. Eventually, in 1995, he overdosed and died, aged 44. "It was very disappointing for me," says Burnham, "because I loved playing with him, and I think he'd have been a good fourth member. Because by this point, certainly from where I was sitting, I felt like it was becoming the Jon and Andy show. I really had very little to do with the writing of the next album, *Songs Of The Free*."

CHAPTER 7

WOMAN TOWN

"People weren't happy, for various reasons. Hugo wasn't happy about not being so involved. Decisions were just not being made as a four-piece any more. Even Andy and Jon were beginning to disagree about things. I guess things were generally falling apart." – Sara Lee

With Dave Allen gone, and Buster Jones having finished his stint as temporary stand-in, Gang Of Four urgently needed a new bassist. They also needed to reconsider what Gang Of Four meant as a band because, as Andy Gill now admits, that original idea of the four-man, all-for-one-and-one-for-all democracy established back in 1977 no longer worked in the current set-up. "The initial idea of *Entertainment!*, with these four blokes in the room arguing it out, had very much changed by this point," says Gill of the period just before the sessions began for the third album, 1982's *Songs Of The Free*. "There's no point trying to call it anything else. Me and Jon were writing the songs, we'd take them into the studio and we'd get people in to play the parts that needed playing. I can't remember who did what on each track now."

A musician called Jon Astrop did indeed play bass on some of the tracks on *Songs Of The Free*, but a more permanent member had been brought into the ranks by then: Sara Lee, who had previously played with Robert Fripp's League Of Gentlemen. Ironically, she was in the studio when she got the call from GOF, recording with ex-XTC keyboardist Barry Andrews – Dave Allen would later form Shriekback with Andrews. She remained Gang Of Four's bass player until their "split" in 1984.

"I loved Barry's music, so I went down to the studio to see him. I think he said something like, 'Oh, come and sing some background vocals'," recalls Lee. "And I was hanging out with them in the studio while they were recording what must have been the first Shriekback record, except maybe they weren't called Shriekback yet. I just remember being in the studio with them, and then Dave arrived to say hello. I guess he and Barry had discussed doing something already and he said to me, 'By the way, you should call the Gang Of Four because they're looking for you.' And that's how I found out about it."

Lee's first impression of the near-mythical punk-funkers was, "I thought they were a bunch of fun-loving guys" – she insists she's being honest, not diplomatic. She does, however, recall GOF being "quite a loose organisation", especially compared with Fripp's tightly controlled LoG, even when they were preparing for her first gig with the band, a big show in a Leeds warehouse in front of 4,000 hardcore GOF-heads.

"It was an incredible experience to be working with Robert Fripp as my first professional job, so I was sort of taken aback by the lack of concern about, you know, playing properly at that gig. Maybe if I'd been in some other punk band I would have thought, 'Oh, this is quite normal.'" Based on their reputation, Lee was perhaps expecting GOF to be more rigorous, disciplined and stern. "Well, I would have expected them to have really made sure that we had the set under our belts and played very well," she says, "although that's not based on any prior knowledge of what they had been like. It's not as though I saw them on stage before and thought, 'Wow, these guys must really work hard at their show.' But just from a professional point of view, I would have expected to have done a bit more rehearsing and spent a bit less time in the pub, but that's such an English thing. Now I live in America and it's so different. People take their craft much more seriously over here than they did in England, certainly in those days in the Eighties.

"But the bottom line is," she hastens to add, "we had a fantastic time rehearsing. I remember thoroughly enjoying it. I thought it was tremendously exciting, and I was really excited about playing with them. It was just a different way of working. It was more about the spirit of the moment, and I loved that. It was a wild time and I really had a lot of fun."

Lee, who comes from a musical family – her parents are music teachers (her father was latterly a bass songman in the choir of York Minster) and her sister is a cellist in the Royal Scottish Symphony Orchestra – also found Gang Of Four a musically invigorating place to be.

"Andy is one of the most exciting guitar players I've ever played with in my life – I love his guitar playing," she enthuses. "To meet this guy who played guitar like that, even though if you asked him to play A-minor he didn't know how to… I thought that was phenomenal. Also, I had to get earplugs pretty quickly! They are one of the loudest bands I've ever played with and I was a little concerned about my hearing."

The band gave Lee *Entertainment!* and *Solid Gold* to learn her parts from, as most of their set around this period was based on the first two albums; soon, they would begin the phase of writing that would lead to *Songs Of The Free*. She found that her "funky, syncopated style" was entirely compatible with the band and provided a seamless segue from Dave Allen. It was exhilarating to be playing 'Armalite Rifle' and the other classic GOF tracks. "It was brilliant," she says. "So powerful." Were Allen's shoes difficult to fill? "Well, Dave was such an integral member, and I definitely felt like I was going into a band," she says. "It was like being hired as a side guy, and there were several other side guys at the time, so there were other musicians in the same boat. But yeah, he'd been such an important member of the band. Luckily, though, my playing style was similar to his so I was able to cope with it.

"But I can completely understand and empathise with Dave from the point of view of being a side person in a band," she adds. "There are inevitably times when the singers, the songwriters, the leaders of the band, do make you feel like they don't take you seriously, they don't respect you, they don't include you. Especially in a band like the Gang Of Four, where it's supposed to be a 'four mates' thing. It can be very frustrating to a musician. Because Andy and Jon were the leaders of the band, and the bass player and the drummer really weren't, in the end. I don't know that they began as an equal four-piece, but certainly by the time I came into it, it wasn't quite like that. But I was never really under any illusion."

Lee denies feeling intimidated by GOF's status as post-punk's foremost politicised intellectuals. "I really wasn't much of a political animal in those days," she admits. "I was more involved in things because of the music than the lyrical content, or even the way that people lived their lives. I never went to university, whereas they all did, and they'd been involved in these political groups and so on. But I really don't remember us sitting around the dressing room having very serious conversations about that stuff, to tell you the truth."

As for the band, they were delighted with the new addition to their ranks. "We did want a woman to help put the band's feminist politics into practice," King told *Musician* magazine. Asked whether the "boys" made a conscious decision to include a woman in the band, King responded: "Well, she actually got the job because we knew her very well and she was a good musician. But at the same time, with her, once she was in the band, it was found to be far more pleasant to have a woman. From that point onwards, we always had two women singing with us – Alyson Williams and Eddi Reader. The two of them became more of the normal scenario."

Lee turned out to be not just a talented bassist but a good vocalist as well, and her vocals helped to give the songs they would soon begin recording for *Songs Of The Free* a melodic and accessible quality, in much the same way that Brix Smith's contributions to The Fall changed that group for the better around the same time.

Lee herself was impressed by GOF's attitude towards women. "I think they were feminists for sure," she says, although there were a couple of occasions when they were "distinctly unfeminist", especially when she found Jon Astrop doing bass parts for *Songs Of The Free* and the fourth album, *Hard*, without her being forewarned. On the whole, though, she and the band had a good working relationship and she "never sensed that I should shut up or they should shut up, or they tried not to say things in front of me or anything like that". Nor did she experience any resistance from hard-core fans who might have preferred Dave Allen on bass. "Not at all," she says. "I remember people being fond of him and saying what a great bass player he was and asking what happened to him. But I certainly don't remember any kind of negative reaction."

Lee even managed to find accommodation with the band's extracurricular activities. "We all used to drink a lot, you know?" she says. "We all used to indulge in various things, but I think that that was happening a lot at that time. There hasn't been anything like that in my life since. But there definitely was in the Eighties."

★ ★ ★

It wasn't long after Lee joined Gang Of Four that they began recording *Songs Of The Free* at Ridge Farm in Capel, Surrey. Although she went down to the studio several times to play her parts, she wasn't really involved in the writing process. But she considers the material for GOF's third album to be strong and to have held up well.

"There were some good songs on that album," she says. "I think that by the time [1983's] *Hard* came around the band was falling apart somewhat. But *Songs Of The Free* still had some of that classic Gang Of Four sound." Her contributions didn't change the shape of the songs, but with her involvement on bass as well as vocals as far back as the demo stage, she does feel she was given ample opportunity to express herself in the studio.

It was the next album, *Hard*, that really saw Gang Of Four trying to play catch-up with the bands they'd influenced in the first place, notably Heaven 17, who had picked up GOF's socialist-funk baton and run with it, commercially speaking. But even on *Songs Of The Free* you get the sense that they were attempting to rectify the damage done by their non-appearance on *Top Of The Pops* for 'At Home He's A Tourist'. "'I Love A Man In Uniform' was the obvious commercially accessible song," Lee agrees of the track that would become their next single. "They [Gill and King] definitely, at some point, decided that they needed to become more commercial if they were going to move ahead of where they'd reached, because I think they'd reached a plateau in terms of number of sales or commercial viability. But that conscious sort of effort happened more on *Hard*, I think, than *Songs Of The Free*, and I always think that that was a big mistake, because I really thought that Gang Of Four were a great band and if they had remained true to their roots I believe their day would have come. Obviously they had a lot of critical acclaim, but I think that they would have gone on to greater things if they'd have stuck to their roots. But that idea of moving closer to those more commercial bands… I don't know that that was really thought about much on *Songs Of The Free*."

With regard to the Gill-King/Burnham dynamic, she says, "It had begun to drift somewhat from what I imagine it was like in the beginning, and that's probably why Dave left when he did. Jon and Andy really did take the reins, but I don't think that's unusual. They were steering everything, and I would imagine Hugo felt a little left out of it, in the same way that Dave would have done. It was just the evolution of the band. It didn't end up being just four people making decisions, and so it was a little strained at times, for sure." Did Lee ever have to act as mediator? "No," she replies. "I really don't think my role was anything like that. Because I was late coming into the band I wasn't as much a member as the other guys had always been, and it was changing by the time I came in, so I didn't try to mediate. I don't remember thinking, 'I could step in here and maybe help relations or help things along', you know? It was more a case of the band being on a certain path... I do remember it being difficult; a sort of uncomfortable feeling. People weren't happy, for various reasons. Hugo probably wasn't happy about not being so involved – decisions were just not being made as a four-piece any more, even more so by the time of *Hard*. By then, Andy was pursuing his own vision of the band. I think he did really want the band to shift, to be more commercially viable, and I'm not sure that that was shared by everybody. By the end, even Andy and Jon were beginning to disagree about things. I guess things were generally falling apart by then." Lee summarises the various characters in the band thus: "Andy's ideas were definitely the ones that prevailed when it came to writing. And Hugo definitely seemed to get more involved on the business side of things, dealing with the record company and stuff. And Jon was really like Andy's partner, on a creative level."

The man chosen to produce *Songs Of The Free* was Mike Howlett, formerly the bassist with prog-rockers/Canterbury Scenesters Gong, as well as one-time member of Strontium 90, the band who became The Police. His previous production credits included The Teardrop Explodes, Orchestral Manoeuvres In The Dark and Tears For Fears. Andy Gill found him easy to work with as well as "highly methodical", which came in handy because the production on GOF's third album was more layered and elaborate than before. Gill and King did all the writing for the album prior to going into the studio, while Burnham was, says Gill, not involved "because he wasn't very interested in that. He wasn't involved in the writing, not because we excluded anybody; it was just one of those things. Dave and Hugo never particularly contributed that much on that side of things. Besides, Hugo had got more involved in the management side of the band, which is what, in later years, he did more of."

The choice of Howlett as producer didn't really register with Lee; suffice it to say that she remarks on the disparity between GOF on record and on stage. "I don't really listen to records I've played on once they've been made," she reveals, "but once in a while I'll put a Gang Of Four record on and it always makes me think, 'Jesus, we were an unbelievably fantastic band.' That must have been one powerful band to go and see. No wonder people went crazy, and we sold out, and places were jammed. It was phenomenal, especially in America."

Around this time, Gang Of Four were performing in the States in front of 5,000-strong audiences. It was just after the Ridge Farm sessions that they played the Roseland Ballroom in New York, to which the fire department and the police had to be called out in force because, despite the venue's capacity having been reached, a further 500 or so punters were massing on the streets outside, desperately trying to squeeze their way in. "It was mayhem," says Lee. "Absolutely incredible."

Not only did Lee have to grow accustomed to GOF's manic crowds, she also had to get used to their on-tour sleeping arrangements, with members having to share hotel bedrooms, even beds, on the road, to keep costs down. Not that she ever had to bunk up with Burnham, Gill or King. "No," she laughs. "I was given the choice of Kevin the sound engineer or Ray the lighting engineer." Before long, she was given a woman to share with – Eddi Reader, then a backing vocalist with the band, later of Fairground Attraction. "I don't think I'd reached the luxury of having my own room yet," she adds. "But I don't want to say anything against the band's wonderful technicians." Eventually, she would shack up with Dave Allen's younger brother Phil, then the band's lighting designer. "I ended up dating Phil for two years, so that took care of that problem," she laughs. "He was a lovely bloke. Really wonderful."

★ ★ ★

According to Garry Mulholland's *Fear Of Music: The 261 Greatest Albums Since Punk And Disco*, *Songs Of The Free*, with its sleeve design courtesy of King and Gill, "looks at America with what could usefully be described as shock and awe." He pinpoints the accessible sound achieved via Mike Howlett's candy-coated production, the conventional pop hooks, crashing drums and reverb-heavy treatment of the instruments as examples of GOF's attempt to broaden their appeal on their third album.

"Here," he writes, "the pressure on the band to write hits to keep their record deal begins to colour their sound, and embodies their analysis of our surrender to consumerism and wage-slavery, with particular emphasis on American economic and military power." Jon King's lyrics, he goes on, "lay bare the inevitable triumph of Thatcher and Reagan's redrawing of our psychology with [a] mordant humour". Their music, meanwhile, "acts out 'the space between our work and its product' examined so brutally and fearfully" on the album's stand-out track, the Joseph Conrad-referencing 'We Live As We Dream, Alone'.

Songs Of The Free, released in May 1982, within months of those other landmarks of subversive, "entryist" New Pop – The Associates' *Sulk*, Scritti Politti's *Songs To Remember* and ABC's *Lexicon Of Love* – does indeed have a commercial sheen, not to mention female backing singers as was then de rigueur, big rock drums and pop melodies. It may have been less inventive, and proved less influential, than *Entertainment!* or even *Solid Gold*, but there's no denying the excellence of 'Call Me Up', 'I Will Be A Good Boy', 'Life! It's A Shame', the brilliant 'We Live As We Dream, Alone' and the single, 'I Love A Man In Uniform'.

"*Songs Of The Free* is a more upbeat dance of death," went one review, while another called it "one of the most stirring, innovative rock albums you can find." *Songs Of The Free* was by no means a pop sell-out. The more elaborate production gave Andy Gill and the other musicians an opportunity to run wild in the studio, overdubbing extra percussion, screeching, careening guitars and all manner of sonic details over the rhythms, which marked a shift from jerky agit-funk to the slick, anti-fascist groove thang then being perfected by Heaven 17.

Andy Gill was certainly in a buoyant mood during this period. "It was a happy time for me," he says, noting that the band were making considerable strides in the States – for one show in Florida at the university, he remembers there being "something like 22,000 people," making it the biggest gig GOF ever played as headliners. But he denies that there was any pressure from the record company to come up with a hit album this time. "No," he says. "The irony of it is that people imagine that independent companies would give you artistic freedom and that the majors would force you to compromise in this way or that way. In my experience, it's the other way around. At no point did anybody at EMI ever say, 'Don't do this' or 'don't do that' or 'you should do this' or 'you should do that'. Nobody ever said anything of the kind at any point. I mean, maybe somebody might pop in during recording, basically to buy us all a drink and chat. But nobody ever said anything about anything in terms of the artwork or the music. We delivered the album, then we'd have a sort of listening party, and everybody would go, 'Oh, yeah, great.' That would be it."

Even within the band, he denies that a more commercial direction was on the agenda. "I think the kinds of things that we do are the things that we do," he says. "With *Entertainment!*, there was a collision between pop culture and some interesting ideas and left-field musical approaches. And that was always part of the project. With 'I Love A Man In Uniform', it's still that same project. It manifests itself in a different way, but it's still the same sort of project."

This project – infiltrating the mainstream with radical, edgy ideas — may have been jinxed. Because no sooner was 'I Love A Man In Uniform' released as a single in May 1982 than Gang Of Four found themselves at the receiving end of a ban by the BBC, just as the song began its journey up the charts. The reason? Britain was about to go to war with the Falklands, and the broadcasting authorities didn't want any songs being aired that appeared to glamorise, or in fact debunk, the military.

"It was going halfway up the charts and getting lots of Radio One plays and all that," recalls Andy Gill, "and then as British ships started approaching Argentina this memo went around the BBC saying, 'Do not play this record under any circumstances. We are expecting casualties in the next 48 hours. This record is banned.' And thanks very much. We hadn't even heard of the fucking Falklands when we wrote 'I Love A Man In Uniform'. Did we feel jinxed? No, it was more like business as usual." As Jon King puts it, "We were banned more than The Sex Pistols."

'I Love A Man In Uniform', with its female soprano mocking a military recruit over a pounding, insistent funk-noir beat, echoed hand-claps and nagging bass, has been described variously as "the flipside to Robert Wyatt's 'Shipbuilding'", "a Falkands protest song", "a subversive dance-rock masterpiece", "a club smash that crossed over to the gay scene" and "the wittiest and most succinct of the band's definitive critiques of male emotional impotence and militarism". Inversion and irony run throughout the melody, as the band recount how the young enlistee has convinced himself that he and his girlfriend were good together, that he was protecting her by joining the army, and that she finds the military romantic. The woman's constant refrain in response to all this is: "You must be joking/Oh man, you must be joking." The joke was, the single sat quite nicely alongside the new New York electro of the period: The Peech Boys' 'Don't Make Me Wait', Dazz Band's 'Let It Whip' and the rest. Notwithstanding the ban and the barbed message, 'I Love A Man In Uniform' got a lot of dance-floor action in the hip nightclubs of the period such as Manchester's Hacienda.

Andy Gill always found the single more amusing than accusatory. "It's a funny song," he says. "It's not all doom and gloom at all." He also reveals it was Gang Of Four's take on contemporary American funk, the kick-drum pattern in particular inspired by the rhythm track to Marvin Gaye's 'Sexual Healing'. "There's something about getting in the car and putting that track on the sound system, you know, loud," he enthuses. "It's not exactly the same, but it was a bit of an inspiration for the feel and the pattern of '… Uniform'." He also believes the single was as influential as it was influenced by Gaye and his keyboard player Odell Brown's music for 'Sexual Healing': Madonna's 2000 hit, 'Music', was, he believes, inspired by GOF's 1982 single. "Whoever was the producer on that [French producer Mirwais] must have listened to 'Man In Uniform'," he says. He could be on to something: even Madonna's reference in her song to "the bourgeosie" is distinctly GOF in tone.

And yet any appeal 'I Love A Man In Uniform' has had over the years has been more of the cult variety, due to the last-minute ban by the BBC. Sara Lee remembers the ban as being, after the 'At Home He's A Tourist' affair, "like some sort of a double-whammy, a second rejection. The timing was dreadful. Were the band disappointed? Yeah, I think so. But the Falklands War just shot everything down in flames."

She believes this second failed bid for mainstream acceptance may have been the reason why American management, under the auspices of a gentleman called Bennett Glotzer, who had looked after, among others, Frank Zappa, was brought in – there was a feeling that, if Gang Of Four were to remain a going concern, they would have to concentrate on the US market. "He was a quintessential Los Angeles music business manager," says Lee. "He had the cigars and the fast cars and the young girls and the cocaine. Put it this way: he wasn't my first choice for managing the band."

Hugo Burnham distinctly recalls EMI being so upset by GOFs second rejection by the British media that the record company began shifting allegiances to another young band with rather greater commercial potential than Gang Of Four. "It was like, 'We've got this new, young group called Duran Duran. We're going to work with them instead.' You know, that other group with short cropped hair and attitude; that other bunch of neo-Marxist intellectuals. It became a big joke, sort of, 'Whatever we do the BBC is gonna fucking ban it', you know? It was almost like, 'Fucking hell, what else is going to happen to us?'"

For Burnham, recording *Songs Of The Free* down in Ridge Farm doesn't have as happy memories as the *Entertainment!* or *Solid Gold* eras. "Not really. We had a new A&R guy, Dave Ambrose, who was an old hippie musician. He was a lovely geezer but I think terribly drug-damaged. I mean, completely not there, with a real 1,000-yard stare. He was very nice and helped out, but... Anyway, we were down in the country in Surrey with chefs and everything in this live-in place, and Mike Howlett, whom I loved, a really lovely guy, we didn't tell him we needed to soften our sound, but I think we probably said in not so many words that we wanted a more professional-sounding record. He used all this new computer technology, which was interesting but I felt was a bit cold at the time. It was all a bit too pleasant – the surroundings, everything."

Burnham also believes there was a simultaneous softening of the band's message on *Songs Of The Free*. "It was subtler, or it had softened along with the music, in a way," he says. "We used to have all these intellectual ideas but we still kicked ass on stage, but we weren't manning the ramparts all the time being dull and boring. We were normal people with rigorous ideas and we were questioning our own ideas and attitudes a lot. We were young people experimenting with how they lived their lives politically. And I don't mean the politics of ideas, I mean the politics of your own actions, how you treat other people and how you analyse things." He accepts, however, that the band had to change if they wanted to achieve greater success. "We really believed in the way we did things and the things we said, but we weren't being terribly successful so we began to question ourselves. We were wondering how to develop things. At that age, you're still learning, and if you're smart, which essentially we were, you adapt your ideas, you change, you develop. When you've been around a little longer, you actually understand that compromise is one of the strongest tools you can bring to any relationship, whether it's a business relationship, a teacher-student relationship or the person you live with and love or otherwise; but a business relationship particularly. And there was not a lot of compromise between us, individually."

Was there a sense in which the four members were trying to make different albums this time? "I don't know. I can't speak for Sara because she came in not as a partner. She was just an employee, really. But, yes, I felt the divide was really beginning here. I wasn't in the studio as much when they were writing as I used to be, and because I was busy with the management side of things before we fixed on Bennett Glotzer as manager. It was like I'd come and tell them what was going on, and it was very much, 'Well, why hasn't it been sorted out yet? How many times have you called? You spoke to them, right?'"

Perhaps Gill and King's short-tempered treatment of Burnham the stand-in manager was the result of frustration that the band were struggling to capitalise on the headway they were making as a serious live proposition. "The venues were getting bigger and bigger and expectations were growing for the band," says Gill. "We were getting really big and selling out big venues. When we put out 'Man In Uniform' in the States, it did really well." He sees no conflict between the band's critiques of capitalism and their desire to make commercial headway. "I don't think I was against making money in the first place," he says. "I've never been against people making money. Being in a band is by its very nature an entrepreneurial thing."

In a free-market economy with Thatcherist, monetarist policies on the rise, did the irony dawn on him that Gang Of Four were model Thatcherites? "That's the kind of theme that Gang Of Four always looked at — what we do to make our lives tick and to make money and…" Expose the contradictions? "Well, there are many contradictions, and Jon and I wouldn't for one millisecond suggest that we shouldn't work in an entrepreneurial fashion. On the one hand you can say, 'It's OK to work for a company because you're a legitimate wage slave and downtrodden', because then the correct relationship between employer and employee is maintained; on the other hand, you can go out and do your own thing and try to make a buck, but then that's seen as entrepreneurial and capitalist, so you're damned if you do…"

It was while Gill and King were wrestling with these contradictions in the studio that Burnham would be manning the phones as a sort of surrogate manager, which seemed like a good use of his time back then but which Gill now considers "kind of created problems − it's not a good idea, generally speaking, to have somebody in the band managing the band. But then, we never quite got around to finding good managers."

Burnham recalls picking up the managerial reins as far back as 1981, "after Linda Neville, who was our second manager and who had been Rob Warr's assistant. We took her on when Rob left because we thought it might give some continuity; plus we loved her, and we thought having a woman manager would be, you know, far out. We were putting ideas before common sense, I think." And so the drummer stepped in. "I took over the day-to-day management just because I'd always been the one hanging out at EMI or Warner Brothers in New York or with our agent, because I liked to see what was going on and how it was done; so while Jon and Andrew were writing I was doing business. I started working with the agent, with the roadies, with the [UK and US] record labels and the publisher, trying to get money. Soon after we finished *Songs Of The Free*, I flew to LA to oversee a club mix of 'I Love A Man In Uniform' and met with Mo Austin and Lenny Waronker, who ran the place [Warner Brothers] and loved Gang Of Four. We weren't making them any money, but they loved us."

It was Warner Brothers' head honchos who tried to warn

Burnham against signing a management deal with Bennett Glotzer. "They said, 'We love the Gang Of Four, we're proud to have you at Warner Brothers, and we will work with anybody. But – and you cannot repeat this outside the room – there are a lot of people at Warner Brothers who will be very, very unhappy if you choose Bennett Glotzer.' Now, I liked him socially but when I returned home to tell Andrew and Jon what Warners had said, it was like waving a flag in a bull's face."

Gill possibly was in an invidious position, faced with a decision as to who to get to manage the band. He didn't particularly trust Glotzer but nor was he entirely comfortable with the notion of the drummer as manager. And so he and King went with Glotzer.

For Sara Lee, this was the beginning of the end. "The whole 'Man In Uniform' era and that tour and the life of that record was great," she says, "and we all seemed to be doing pretty well, but by the time *Hard* came around, it began to deteriorate. With personalities clashing and the way the band was being run, it started to get less enjoyable. It was a shame, because it was a band that started off as four equal partners, and it was just disintegrating on that level, the hierarchical structure or whatever…"

Burnham puts it most succinctly. "I really felt the divide setting in when Bennett Glotzer came in as manager," he says. "And then two months later I was out."

CHAPTER 8

SHEER HARD ATTACK

"If I'd have liked Hard, I think I might have killed myself."
– Hugo Burnham.

Although arguments among the various members of Gang Of Four had been commonplace virtually since the band's inception in 1977, with Hugo Burnham the band member most likely to be at odds with Jon King or Andy Gill, the drummer was still taken absolutely by surprise when he was given the bad news. It was following a particularly gruelling European tour in 1983 that culminated with a gig in Germany that was filmed for German music TV show *Rockpalast*.

"I didn't know it, but that was my last Gang Of Four gig for 20-odd years," recalls Burnham. "We got back to England and then, a week later, I was told by Andy or Jon, 'OK, now we need to talk.' So I went to a meeting at Andy's place in London and I was kicked out. Jon just said, 'I'm sick of arguing about everything.' And so I was gone. How did I feel? Fucking devastated, frankly. A wiser, older man might have seen it coming. Stupid, really. But that's OK. It had been a different thing since *Songs Of The Free* anyway. We'd fired our management and I was left with the somewhat unenviable task of managing the band. It was probably time."

Gill draws a distinction, regarding band relations, between Gang Of Four before and after their second album, *Solid Gold*. "After *Solid Gold* it became a slightly different arrangement," he considers. "Then the cracks in this rather fanciful construction of a democratic unit that we erected for ourselves became sort of gaping." According to Gill, Burnham's managerial role "wasn't going well" and "caused a bit of friction between him, me and Jon". He adds that Burnham always thought of him as "the enemy".

"Even in the old days," he says, "Hugo and I never particularly liked each other. But I thought we were happy just to co-exist, and go for a drink. I didn't particularly seek out his company, but we'd share a joke when no one else was in the room, and get along."

Burnham didn't realise that the heated internal arguments were proving too much to bear for Gill and King, and they used this as the rationale for ousting him and wresting control of the band. "For me the arguing was just part of the process. You rack things out and you come to a decision. But I think Jon and Andy wanted a duopoly rather than a triumvirate. They wanted to have their way with things and just have a rhythm section that was paid to do as they were told." Burnham doesn't remember there being too much of a debate about the matter. "Really," he says, "I was a bit too stunned. I was just like, 'Oh, all right. I get to keep all my drums, though, don't I?'"

Sara Lee wasn't at the final meeting because "she was a paid-to-play member, not a voting member"; instead, present were just Burnham and the two other original GOF members, whom the drummer, despite being in a state of shock, went to see play "a couple of times" over the next year or so "because I still loved the band". One gig in particular, at London's Lyceum, Burnham found especially distressing. He'd been given a backstage pass, so he sat at the side of the stage and watched them perform. Trouble was, his presence proved so unsettling for replacement sticksman Steve Goulding that he was asked to leave. "The roadies said, 'You're freaking Steve out. Can you go away?' So I left. I just walked out.

Suddenly it dawned on me what had really happened. It was very traumatic, like the end of a long relationship, although the difference was that most relationships take a bit of time to end. There was no make-up sex on this one. But don't ask me to comment on *Hard*. Put it this way: it was not another great Gang Of Four record."

The last album to bear Gang Of Four's name before their dissolution in 1984, *Hard*, their fourth long-player, was the first to feature just Gill and King of the original line-up, even if Burnham did play on a few demos for the record. Not that he was all that bothered about having been ejected prior to its completion once he heard the finished product. "I didn't think that was a terribly good album," he says. "It gave me pleasure not to like it. It was a misnomer of a record: I mean, 'hard' it wasn't. It was ghastly. There were a couple of good songs, but really it was not the Gang Of Four. It was all a bit Heaven 17-ish. And the videos were awful: terrible clothes and terrible hair. I laughed when I saw them. I was still mourning it really, so I guess I was predisposed not to like it. So it made it a lot easier when I really *didn't* like it. If I'd have liked *Hard*, I think I might have killed myself."

Hard is generally regarded as the last proper Gang Of Four album, despite there being two more that followed it, probably because it preceded the announcement of the band's split. Recorded at the Hit Factory studios in Miami, Florida, it is also routinely described as the nadir of their career. "Considering where they'd come from, *Hard* wasn't just a let-down, it was an outright travesty," wrote one critic later on, while another was even more incensed by what he heard on their 1983 album. "*Hard* is nothing more than a grotesque exhibition of a once-great band on its last legs." Opined *Melody Maker*'s Lynden Barber, "*Hard* is largely a string of wasted opportunities." He added that "the Gang simply sound old". Meanwhile, *Rolling Stone*'s David Fricke, such an ardent champion of *Entertainment!*, called the album "a bland offering of Manhattan disco with dashes of post-punk cool".

Whatever you thought of the content, there's no denying that *Hard* was a curious title for an album that saw the band smoothing the edges and softening the surfaces of their sound. "The would-be ironic title wound up a joke King and Gill played on themselves; in execution and content, the album is anything but its namesake," declared another reviewer. The same critic took issue with King's vocals – "He sounds utterly disinterested at almost every turn, the urgency of his old, oft-imitated declamatory style completely lost, as he allows himself to become a conventional singer" – as well as with the blandly soulful female backing vocalists, including Chic's Alfa Anderson, who open the album chanting, "Is it love?" ("So overproduced, they sound practically synthesized"), and found fault with the rhythms ("the drum programming is straight-up Oingo Boingo"). The only positive aspects of the album that critics pointed to were the club-friendly grooves, the hook-laden melodies and Andy Gill's guitar parts, which, although not as incendiary and confrontational as before, still seemed to assault the listener through the speakers. Closer retroactive inspection of *Hard* reveals an enjoyable collection – albeit one somewhat enervated compared with the high-energy invention displayed on *Entertainment!*, and suffused with the sad realisation that you can't turn Marxist analysis into chart pop – of polished, rocked-up synth-funk, the sort that was prevalent at the time.

The accusation most frequently levelled at Gang Of Four around the release of *Hard* was that they were "selling out"; that they were deliberately, even cynically, trying to appeal to a bigger audience and turning their backs on their hard-core fans. They certainly chose producers with a successful track record, even if the field those producers had previously operated in couldn't have been further removed from Gang Of Four's post-punk-funk terrain: Ron and Howard Albert, who had been recording engineers on albums by Derek & The Dominos, The Allman Brothers and Crosby, Stills & Nash.

"There are things that I really like about that record, but I think that it slightly fails," says Gill of *Hard*. "The producers weren't right for it. Things weren't great. We had come to a rather bad point because we were being managed by Bennett Glotzer, who had managed Frank Zappa and was from the old school. I wasn't exactly a fan of his: he created massive problems."

Gill's preferred choice of producer to work on *Hard* was Nile Rodgers, one half, along with Bernard Edwards, of disco super-team Chic and at that time the world's hottest studio whiz, with David Bowie's *Let's Dance* on his list of credits and Madonna poised to invite him to collaborate with her on her second album, *Like A Virgin*. Trouble was, Glotzer got involved in the financial negotiations and scuppered the plan. "We were regularly in contact with Nile about it," the guitarist remembers, "and then, suddenly, he wasn't doing it any more. It turns out Bennett Glotzer had quibbled over half a percentage point in terms of the royalties, either with Nile or with Nile's management." Gill was disappointed to say the least. "I couldn't fucking believe it. Glotzer did it. He said, 'Sorry Andy, it's not going to happen.' But it was going to happen until the dispute over the royalties. I said, 'You're fucking insane.' After that, my heart wasn't in it."

Gill met further resistance during the recording of *Hard* when he faced arguments with the others over the sound he wanted to achieve for the album. "I wanted to use electronic stuff but other people, including Sara Lee, argued against me, saying, 'Why use a synthesizer when you can use a real orchestra?' And I didn't stick to my guns. I didn't really want a real horn section and string players. That wasn't the sound that I wanted, you know? But that's what we ended up with."

Although it was recorded in the States, the writing and demoing of the material for *Hard* took place in a studio in London's Mount Pleasant district, at the crossroads between Clerkenwell Road and Gray's Inn Road. "We locked ourselves in there for months," recalls Gill. "It was basically me and Jon, plus some drum machines, percussion and keyboards. Actually, that's how *Songs Of The Free* was done as well."

Nevertheless, by the time the Albert brothers were drafted in, Gill had been wrong-footed. "Pretty much all of that record was done in the wrong way," he says, "and I blame Bennett Glotzer. It's easy to say now, but when that whole thing with Nile Rodgers fell through because of our fucking manager, we should have just stopped and regrouped. It was a mistake to power ahead with it, to just do it because we thought we were ready. And then we went with this totally inappropriate pair of producers. We were sort of walking around in a daze. It was like, 'Let's get a string section on this.' 'Well, I'd rather use a synthesizer.' I just felt it wasn't going the right way." Gill does cite 'A Man With A Good Car' and 'Woman Town' – the latter about the power play between men and women and sexual politics in general – as good tracks. He just didn't like the album's overall sound, the "general feel"; he wanted something "hard and funky". Problem was, he felt undermined by "the management", leading to a loss of motivation and that all-important creative energy.

Sara Lee agrees with Gill that the Albert brothers were the wrong choice as producers for *Hard*. "They were very much Miami, Florida guys," she says. "It's a shame that they [the band] didn't have more cutting-edge producers at that time – and I'm including Mike Howlett here – because I think they went a bit too soft and smooth around the edges." The bassist can appreciate some of the songs on the album, citing 'Silver Lining' as her favourite, but she was bemused by Gill's decision to take the lead vocal on some of the tracks, notably 'Woman Town', and imagines that this might have been indicative of a desire on his part to assume the lead role in Gang Of Four.

"I didn't really know why he wanted to sing, to be honest," she says. "I mean, I can understand anybody wanting to sing, but maybe in Andy's case he really was trying to change the direction of the band. But I think it's a shame that it wasn't Jon doing the singing."

Gill had, admits Lee, become "quite controlling" by this point. "His ego got out of control," she says. "At the time I was very upset about it. But of course I didn't have as much invested in it as the other guys did, so it's a completely different experience for me. It was just a band that I played with, and I've played with so many other bands since. And it's very rare that you meet a band where everybody's compatible and happy about the way everything's being run. But, you know, it was 25 years ago, and we were so much younger and so much more inexperienced than we are now."

Burnham talks about Gill just prior to his departure from the band as something of a tyrant. Lee, too, remembers that Gill wanted to get involved in every aspect of performing and recording. "It did get pretty bad," she reveals. "I don't know why Andy ended up being so sort of extreme about it, taking lead vocals, and then also playing drums and doing drum overdubs that took days in the studio. I remember being in Miami and the drum overdubs just seemed to go on and on, and I was just lying by the pool, which I wasn't complaining about, but…

"Andy is a very talented musician and guitarist, and you get that kind of behaviour with a lot of talented people," Lee continues. "And I can sometimes forgive it. Not that I want to be around it necessarily or work with people who do that kind of thing, but sometimes people are not really very thoughtful about other people when they're in there [i.e. the studio] creating their art. They don't think, 'I wonder if I'm upsetting the other members of the band?' They're just thinking, 'I want to do it like this. I'm going to do it like this.' But given that this was meant to be a four-piece band, I thought it was a shame that it disintegrated like that. I think they lost the plot, you know?"

According to Lee, the decision to oust Burnham was not for commercial reasons but simply due to personal differences. "It wasn't because they [Gill and King] felt he was holding them back. I think it was personality clashes at that point. I don't think they were looking at him thinking, 'Wow, we could be really commercial if we had a different drummer.' It was just personalities." She believes Gill had such specific designs for the sound of *Hard* that it wasn't just Burnham who suffered; sometimes even Gill's ally King felt isolated. "It wasn't just the bass player and the drummer who were moved to one side," she says. "It became Jon as well. I remember him saying to me that he just didn't understand what Andy was trying to do. I think it was hard for Jon to understand why he wasn't singing lead on some of the songs."

As for her own position, often Lee would find her bass parts handed over to session player Jon Astrop without any warning or explanation, which was difficult for her to accept and indicative of the deterioration in inter-band relations. "By then I was probably having a hard time because of the way some of the recordings were going. I was beginning to get disillusioned. In fact, when the band broke up finally in 1984, I did feel that I should have left a few months earlier. I wasn't enjoying being on the road and playing so much. They also replaced me without telling me on at least one of the songs on *Hard*: Jon Astrop on 'Is It Love?'. I went into the studio one day and there he was. They hadn't even told me that he was going to be doing it." Turns out Gill wanted a slap-bass approach for 'Is It Love?' in the vein of the then-popular Mark King of Level 42, a style Lee felt unable, or unwilling, to replicate. "I just had no desire to play like that – it didn't feel like bass to me," she says, adding that she felt "really upset and hurt" when Astrop replaced her on that track. "I felt at least they should have been honest and said to me, 'You know what? We really want to have this particular style of bass-playing on this one song, so we'd like to use Jon.' I would have said, 'Well, fine. I totally understand. Go ahead.'" Instead, there was no prior warning. "I walked in on it and they hadn't said anything. It was horrible. I just felt they didn't treat me very well over that issue. I wish they'd just been upfront about it: I really don't think I would have minded. But to be done behind my back when I was supposed to be a member of the band... I'm sure Hugo and Dave felt the same way as me, only much more so, because they were supposed to be proper full-time members of the band but it was slipping away from them."

Gill regrets making Lee feel uncomfortable by using Astrop without explaining it to her first. "It was a bit problematic, but I felt that Jon [Astrop] played some of those parts in a way that suited the song better, and that's never going to go down well. We just tried to reach a compromise on it and move on, you know? But I'm sure she wasn't very happy about it, and maybe in retrospect it wasn't a great idea − well, musically it might have been, but it wasn't necessarily good for the band's morale." He compares the fluid approach to musicians adopted by Gang Of Four during the *Hard* era to the strategy employed by Talking Heads, with Tina Weymouth often replaced on songs by GOF's one-time bassist Busta Jones. On the whole, though, he feels that Lee was "great for the band". How did her presence change the band dynamic? "I think people probably got on a bit better than they had done before. I enjoyed being around this bunch of people and really felt kind of bonded, which wasn't always the case in the 'classic' Gang Of Four."

Considering their music dissected the minutiae of inter-personal relations, did Gill acknowledge the irony of watching the band fall apart, even as they wrote songs that critically examined the flawed nature of the human condition? "Well, when you form a group, no matter what you're doing, it emerges; your projects emerge as you go about being in a group," he explains. "You don't start a group with a blueprint, because you don't know what you're doing. You don't have a clue, so you work out what you're doing as you go along. But yes, the mechanics and the politics of how you arrange your structure to make the product are things that we took as a subject matter. But the one thing about Gang Of Four that marks us out from other people with a very political bent is that we never have suggested that we're not 'collaborators'. We recognise that we're 'collaborators', and the whole idea of us being on the righteous side of the fence, waving the righteous flag and pointing at the people who were in the wrong, was always alien to us. We always laughed at that form of 'rock rebellion'." Gill actually wrote a song once, 'The Producer', about the band dynamic, about "who did what" in the studio. Did he ever find it frustrating that GOF could create this incredibly sophisticated framework of ideas and yet were unable to distance themselves from, and soberly reach a compromise on, the very things they wrote about? "No," says Gill, "because then I could say to Jon, 'See, told you that was going to happen!'"

Ultimately, Gill is just happy to have produced a body of work that functions on two levels: it provides a narrative of the band's career, as well as telling a parallel story about the evolution of rock from punk, through post-punk and beyond to the New Pop era. "They [GOF's records] sort of tell a story about pop. I think that's a good way of putting it."

★　★　★

That story came to an end in 1984, reaching a climax at a series of American shows recorded for posterity on the *At The Palace* live album, released by Mercury Records, also in 1984.

Gang Of Four had, as usual, been spending quite a bit of time in America on tour. And although the buzz wasn't quite what it once was, compared with their first-ever tour of the States – when, according to Andy Gill, "Your eyes are pretty wide open and it's a new experience and it's enormously exciting" – the thrill was still there. R.E.M. would often be GOF's support band, or rather, now that R.E.M. were growing in popularity, the positions would be reversed. Sometimes they'd find themselves by chance in the same town, playing gigs at different venues, and Gill or Jon King would get a call to go and join Michael Stipe and co for an encore – a version of The Velvet Underground's 'Sweet Jane', say, or even GOF's own 'We Live As We Dream, Alone'. Occasionally, there would be joint nights out, fairly heavy sessions with Athens,

Georgia's finest that, as Gill hazily recalls, "Would be memorable if I could remember them".

On the whole, though, life on the road during the *Hard* era wasn't as exciting as before, and at some point Gill and King decided that now might be a good time for the band to take some time off and reconsider their position.

"I think when we were out on the road with *Hard*," recalls Gill, "me and Jon had the chat and just said, 'We should just give it a rest for a while.' I don't think we were saying, 'Let's not ever do this again.' It just meant, 'Let's give it a rest for a while.'"

"The Gang Of Four have called it a day, due to musical differences," *Melody Maker* reported in March 1984. The music weekly claimed that the group held a farewell performance at London's Hammersmith Palais, a show that apparently saw the original line-up briefly in place once more, as Dave Allen and Hugo Burnham joined Gill and King during one of the encores. But no one in the band can actually remember that London gig. Instead, it's GOF's final shows at the Palace Theater in Hollywood that remain etched on the musicians' memories.

"Oh, boy. How can I not remember that?" says Sara Lee. "Those shows were incredible." She points out, correctly, that there were two further "final" shows in Sacramento, but it's the Palace dates that, for her and everyone else still involved, marked the end of the line. "Of all the places to end a band: Sacramento," she laughs, adding, "I did feel numb by the end. I couldn't believe that it was ending, but by then I felt that I shouldn't be in the band, really. It was too hard by that point. Nonetheless, it was such an amazing era, and it was such a great band – and such a shame that it ended like that. I do remember that last night at the Hollywood Palace: it was a great show. I never talked to Jon about it, but I think he was probably feeling, like everybody was, that it was time to call it a day."

Lee can remember King and Gill being "very pally" towards the end, not to mention quite sad. As for the bassist herself, she was "nearly crying during the last show, just because I couldn't believe that it was the last time I was going to be playing these songs." It was around this time that she moved to America, so after the Palace gigs she didn't see the others again for years: there was no sense of closure, which she regrets. "It would have been good to sit down after it all and chat over a cup of coffee. That would have been nice."

There was plenty they could have discussed. Like the all-night drink and drug binges almost everyone in the band indulged in. "We would regularly be up till eight in the morning, all over America," she reveals, adding, "It wasn't anything really nasty – not that coke's not nasty, but there was nothing else. Not that I knew of, anyway. I mean, maybe people were doing anti-depressants on the side..." Nevertheless, it was fairly full-on, she admits, as she reminisces about her entrée into GOF's world. "Oh God, that band was unbelievable. I couldn't believe the first show I did with them, the amount of alcohol that was in the dressing room. There were 72 cans of beer – three crates or something – for the four of us and the crew, plus, I think, three or four bottles of wine, a bottle of vodka, a bottle of Kahlua, and a bottle of bourbon. That was every night – that was the rider." How much would be left by the end of the night? "Nothing," she replies. "Now, obviously, there were friends, there were fans, there were hangers-on, there was management, there was press, there were the people you'd always find backstage. But it was a pretty full-on situation all round. I sometimes think that all of that was what made the band what it was. They were incredible – this wasn't a bunch of calm, politically correct guys sitting around and then just walking on stage and playing a few songs. It was a lifestyle. This was a wild bunch of people, having an incredible time out on the road, playing music every night, travelling around Europe and America and enjoying everything, you know? It was just the way we lived. We were all in our early twenties and everybody was living life to its fullest."

Lee is amused by the band's reputation for puritanical abstention. "Puritanical is probably the other end of the spectrum from what they were. It wasn't that people were completely out of control, ending up in hospital and having sex with 25 students at once or anything like that. It wasn't like that. There weren't groupies on the bus or anything. I've been on other jobs where someone will take a groupie – some poor, innocent girl who doesn't know what she's doing – onto the bus, but we never did that. That wasn't the band; that wasn't what people were interested in." She recalls one occasion when manager Bennett Glotzer hired a stripper for Jon King's birthday while they were recording in a studio somewhere in America, and the singer was mortified. "He was very uncomfortable: you could see Jon's true colours. He wanted to get the girl out of the room as quickly as possible, basically. He did not appreciate that at all." GOF's favourite tipple wasn't women, then, it was booze. "Yeah, that was the way to go. It wasn't hurting anybody else. It was just killing ourselves."

Chris Briggs, the band's former A&R man at EMI, who left the company soon after the release of *Entertainment!*, was working for Mercury in 1984, and it was he who oversaw the production and release of the *At The Palace* live album. "They'd decided to break up and the idea was to do a live album to close that chapter," he says. The atmosphere at the Palace was, he recalls, "pretty mad", with Gill feeling ill and under pressure. In fact, Briggs had to drive the guitarist down to a hospital in Santa Monica after the latter sprained his ankle in a fall, and there were doubts that he'd be able to perform. "It was crazy, and slightly chaotic – Westlife it wasn't," says Briggs. "And there was some sadness, but I don't want to be too showbiz about it. There was a lot of pissed-offness."

Briggs himself was disappointed that the band never realised all their potential, having originally "imagined them as a huge band, doing something different and new, reinventing it all, playing to big audiences live." For him, the *Top Of The Pops*/'At Home He's A Tourist' debacle wasn't the be-all-and-end-all because he didn't see them as a big pop group; rather, he envisioned for them the sort of future soon to be enjoyed by R.E.M.: a big, adult rock band with a huge live following and steady album sales. Nor did he see his presence at the Palace shows as an opportunity to keep the band together. "If band members fall out, that's their problem," he says. "I don't feel I have to nursemaid other people's relationships. They'd already decided to break up. Then they came to me about the live album."

Briggs also regrets the disintegration of the original four-piece. "You always want John, Paul, George and Ringo," he says, "even if it's just for sentimental reasons. But it just wasn't possible in that context. Things were already quite advanced. The relationship between Andy and Hugo had always been volatile, from the start. By the end, though, it wasn't so much hideous as... resigned." Nevertheless, for Briggs, his two stints with Gang Of Four remain a highlight of his career. "Of anyone I've ever worked with, they stand out – and that's not just showbiz bullshit," he says. "They were so bright. Because of the earnestness of their initial presentation, people miss how funny and sharp they were: they were darkly, sharply funny, and always rubbing up against each other from day one. They were all very strong characters. It was a big highlight for me – all the reasons you want to be in this business were there. The only thing that didn't happen was the huge success, which might have made it difficult for neo-Trotskyists to deal with and given them another ghastly contradiction to wrestle with. But it would have been a good excuse for a pint. In fact, that's what Gang Of Four were – a good excuse for an intellectual row down the pub!"

Andy Gill doesn't recall the Palace shows being "particularly super-emotional". He remembers mixing the album in London over a period of a couple of weeks, an exacting operation that removed a lot of the emotion from the situation. But then, he had other things on his mind at the time: at the age of 27, he had just been diagnosed with cancer. "At the beginning of that tour I'd been diagnosed with testicular cancer," he reveals. "But I played the tour anyway and went straight into hospital afterwards, to the Mount Sinai hospital in New York." Having felt pain in one of his testicles, Gill visited a doctor, only to be told that he had a tumour. So he had it removed and was laid up in bed for over a month. "They removed the bollock – or testis, to use the medical term," he jokes. "They do it differently in America – they cut you open and pull out loads of nymph nodes to check them, because that's the next place it [the cancer] goes. We hit that wall entirely fine, but the operation took me five weeks to recover from. I've got a scar from here to here," he points at a large area above the groin. "It was like getting hit by a truck. When I came round I couldn't fucking believe it. I never knew what pain was until I came round from that. They put me on a pretty fucking heavy morphine drip, but the first 24 hours were unbelievable."

Luckily, Gill found just the right remedy for his ills: several weeks in a recording studio with a bunch of wild young LA boys and fanatical Gang Of Four acolytes called The Red Hot Chili Peppers.

CHAPTER 9

INDEPENDENCE

"It was a shock to the system" – Andy Gill.

L ife after Gang Of Four was good, and busy, for Dave Allen. In 1982, the bassist formed Shriekback with Barry Andrews, formerly of XTC and League Of Gentlemen, on keyboards, synthesizers and vocals, and Carl Marsh on guitars and vocals. Shriekback may not have had the critical impact of Allen's first band, but they enjoyed some success in the clubs with their debut release, 'My Spine (Is The Bassline)', and reached the UK Top 60 with the 1984 single 'Hand On My Heart'. In the States, their best-known song, 'Nemesis', received considerable airplay on the indie/college circuit, and remains the only song in the rock pantheon to include the word "parthenogenesis" as part of its chorus. Director Michael Mann was such a fan of Shriekback that he used several of their songs in his films *Manhunter* and *Band Of The Hand*.

After leaving Shriekback, Allen formed rock band King Swamp in 1988, the year he moved to America. He later became an indie music entrepreneur: between 1989 and 1996, his World Domination Recordings, which he founded, released records by artists such as Low Pop Suicide, The Elastic Purejoy, Stanford Prison Experiment, Perfume Tree, Sky Cries Mary, Loop Guru, Sugar Plant and Noah Stone, and published a fanzine featuring his own essays. Despite an ambitious plan to release a work of 20 volumes, instead he issued the soundtrack to the 1993 thriller *The Harvest* and The Elastic Purejoy's *The Clutter Of Pop And Talk Radio* album.

Subsequently, Allen was made director of Consumer Digital Audio Services at Intel in Portland, Oregon, before becoming the president of the entertainment division of the Overland Agency, an advertising firm also based in Portland. Today, he is part of a company called Nemo Design and runs the independent record label Pampelmoose, which specialises in digital-music distribution and brand marketing. Following a period in Los Angeles, he has for several years lived with his wife and children in Portland, where he is something of a local celebrity.

After leaving Gang Of Four in 1983, Hugo Burnham worked as an occasional session drummer with Nona Hendryx, Nikki Sudden, ABC (he appeared in the video for their 1983 hit 'That Was Then, This Is Now' and, encouraged by former GOF manager and then ABC manager Rob Warr, toured Japan, Australia and America with the group) and PiL. He finally made it onto *Top Of The Pops* when he performed on the last named's 1986 hit 'Rise' alongside Bruce Smith, former drummer with The Pop Group and The Slits. Bizarrely, he was also drummer-for-hire for former Page 3 "stunna" Samantha Fox, whose debut hit, 'Touch Me (I Want Your Body)', coincidentally co-written by sometime Gang Of Four bassist Jon Astrop, saw Burnham back on *Top Of The Pops* within weeks. "It was a lot of fun," he says, adding: "A man's gotta make a living." It was Astrop who got Burnham the Fox gig after seeing him drumming on PiL's 'Rise'. Recalls Burnham: "He was like, 'God, man, that was great, it was so cool,' and I said, 'Yeah, yeah, it was great.' He said, 'I've got something even cooler for you.' And then I said, 'Oh, wow, great. Who is it?' He said, 'Samantha Fox.' I didn't miss a beat. I said, 'Yeah, fucking cool. I'll do it.'" Burnham thoroughly enjoyed the experience. "She [Fox] was great. Her dad was managing her, and I worked with them on and off for four or five months, going to Europe, doing TV shows and appearances and all those sorts of things. And I have to tell you they treated me so well. I never had to wait to be paid or felt like, 'Back of the bus, you.' It was quite an uplifting time for me. It made me feel better."

Around this time Burnham joined his former GOF bandmate Dave Allen in Shriekback, serving as that band's manager from 1985 until 1988 and joining in their "slightly unsavoury but enormously fun" on-the-road antics. "We had a blast," he says, "because Shriekback were a fantastic live band, really awesome. We went to Japan and Australia, which Gang Of Four had never been to and where I made friends with Michael Hutchence of INXS, who were big Gang Of Four fans."

In the Nineties he moved from London to New York to open an office for his company, Huge & Jolly Management. He subsequently worked as an A&R executive with Island Records in New York, Imago Records in New York and Los Angeles, Qwest Records in Los Angeles (where label boss Quincy Jones told him, "You can do all that noisy white shit that I don't understand"), and finally EMI Music Publishing in Los Angeles, where he met his wife, Carol, who was head of publicity at Capricorn Records. He reunited briefly with Allen to play on The Call leader Michael Been's solo album, *On The Verge Of A Nervous Breakdown*. After leaving EMI, he returned to artist management with Deathray, then left Los Angeles for Gloucester, Massachusetts at the end of 1998, adding Little Red Rocket and Boston rock group C60 to his roster.

By this point, Burnham was feeling disillusioned with the music industry and, with a new baby, had to supplement his income with work on a building site while his wife worked part-time in Starbucks. "The year before that, between the two of us we'd been pulling down over a quarter of a million dollars [annually] in LA," he reveals. "Suddenly that went down to about $25,000 over the next three or four years. We went through our savings – having a baby without health insurance is fucking expensive over here – but we crawled back, and I got this teaching gig through an old friend of mine who used to manage Squeeze. He said, 'I've got a great job at this college teaching about the music industry. You'd be great for that. Come and meet my boss.' So I did. I got one class, and it snowballed from there. I had to promise them I'd get my master's degree in education, which I did, because I'd only got my bachelor's. And my wife, who used to be a dancer before we were married, became a Pilates instructor, teaching the other teachers how to do it. Together, we scraped out new lives and careers for ourselves. Today, I run the whole freshman seminar department at the New England Institute of Art in Boston."

Jon King also stayed in the music business following Gang Of Four's demise: he had stints in bands called Mechanic Creature and King Butcher, to little acclaim or attention. He wrote a lot of music for TV and film, notably the title music for the BBC's *Pandora's Box*, and co-wrote songs that featured on the soundtracks of major movies such as *The Karate Kid* (1984), *The Manchurian Candidate* (2004) and *Marie Antoinette* (2006).

In the Nineties, after years critiquing the media, King got a job in the media: he is currently the chief executive of World Television, which produces news reports, webcasts and corporate videos for clients from Greenpeace to Nestlé. Before that he developed the British Satellite News service targeted at the Arab and Islamic world for the British Government's Foreign Commonwealth Office; prior to that, he was head of European Business for ScreenRed, a division of John Ryan International, providing strategic content consultancy and integrated screen-based communications and technology solutions in the retail sector. As a main board director of the Mar-Com group, he set up Convergent Technology Solutions to provide strategic consultancy for the delivery of media solutions across networks and the Internet for clients such as Ericsson and Deutsche Bank. Only someone as astute, incisive and media-savvy as Jon King could make the transition from rock frontman to cyber guru; only a band like Gang Of Four could contain a lyricist capable of making that leap.

Andy Gill is the only member of Gang Of Four who has never worked outside the music business. He spent the first few years following GOF's split busily working on other bands' music, most notably a new American funk-rock outfit from California called The Red Hot Chili Peppers, whose self-titled debut album he produced in 1984. Unfortunately, the relationship between the fledgling funk-rockers and their mentor wasn't quite as smooth as it might have been. It was reported that the band and producer fought over creative issues, with Gill allegedly directing them towards a more radio-friendly sound. According to rumour and hearsay, when the band heard *The Red Hot Chili Peppers*, they were so disappointed with the sound that they sent Gill a pizza box containing nothing but a steaming lump of faeces.

"If you want to hear what shaped the sound of the rookie Red Hot Chili Peppers, put that record on the turntable," bassist Michael "Flea" Balzary has said of *Entertainment!*, giving the reasons for wanting Gill at the controls of the Chilis' debut album. "When we made our first record, we just wanted to go in and rock, so we got Andy Gill to produce it. That was great up to a point – but we were aggressively immature and obnoxious about getting what we wanted, and not knowing how to get it and freaking out when we didn't get it, so it kind of ruined that relationship with him. We didn't know how to deal with him and he didn't know how to deal with us. But it was so exciting for me at the time to hang out with him. That record was a big mistake, but I still love Gang Of Four, and I still listen to them. In fact, my daughter started playing drums recently – she plays in a band called The Tints – and the first thing I played her was Gang Of Four. I told her to learn those beats, because they were so great."

Gill is sanguine about his involvement with the Chili Peppers. "It was quite an experience – not all of it good, not all of it bad," he says. "At one point I sent Anthony [Kiedis] off for vocal lessons to try to get him to do something in tune. He came back a better singer – he's actually not bad at it now. But really, they were just young lads getting in the studio for the first time and doing loads of drugs: as far as I know, that meant speed, coke and smack. Anthony would disappear for days at a time. I didn't feel the need to say anything – as long as I could get on with the guitars and whatever needed doing. As long as I wasn't held up, I wasn't that bothered, you know?"

He remembers the Chilis giving their former guitarist, Jack Sherman, a hard time for his esoteric areas of interest. "He was a macrobiotic, and slightly hick-ish, and they gave him absolute fucking hell. In fact, he tried to sue them for emotional damage – he took them to court, although he didn't win. I saw them at gigs where Flea and Anthony would just take the piss out of him. But he was a brilliant guitarist, and he was the one that introduced the band to Parliament and Funkadelic – whatever anyone else says, that was totally down to Jack Sherman."

While Sherman provided some steady musicianship in the studio, mercurial frontman Kiedis would be unpredictable to say the least. "Various interesting things happened," teases Gill. "Like, Anthony would go missing for two or three days at a time – it was a drug thing. Once, when I was in the studio recording a song called 'True Men Don't Kill Coyotes', I thought it would be brilliant to have an acoustic guitar strumming throughout the track, so Jack started playing it. Suddenly, halfway through a take, the door opens and Anthony comes in, and he's standing there for about 30 seconds, and he goes, 'Is that an acoustic guitar I'm hearing?' And I'm like, 'Yeah, it's good, isn't it?' And he goes, 'No fucking acoustic guitar on my fucking record!' He pulls the door open, goes into the live room, rips the guitar off of Jack, smashes it on the floor, and walks off. So we got another one out and carried on. Funnily enough, when the album came out, he liked it and had forgotten about the incident. But at the time it was just, 'Acoustic guitar? That's not punk rock.'"

So how about that pizza box incident – is it an urban myth or true? The circumstances are correct, if not the reasons for it, says

Gill. "We were mixing at the El Dorado studio, which had been there in the centre of Hollywood since the Forties and Fifties. Again, we hadn't seen Anthony for a while when suddenly the door opens and in he comes, with Flea this time, who says, 'We're going to go and take a shit now.' I'm like, 'Great. Bring me one back.' And then they left the room. I thought, 'Why the fuck did I say that? Shit.' I knew a split second later that I shouldn't have – I knew what was going to happen next, without any question. Because, of course, five minutes later they had a couple of pizza boxes, which they put down on the desk... The engineer just ran off like a cartoon – you know, Speedy Gonzalez. He was last seen running down Sunset Boulevard, screaming his head off. What did I say? 'That's very nice. Can you take it away now, please?' They were in hysterics. It was the funniest thing they'd ever seen."

Gill denies that it had anything to do with bad feelings about the production sound on their album. "No, they just wanted their guitar hero to come and hang out with them, spread good vibes and go, 'Yeah, that's fucking great.' But I took it seriously and wanted to do a good job." Apparently, the band wanted to carry on doing their super-fast, two-minute punk-rock tunes, while Gill was encouraging them to do the sort of slower funk-rock numbers with rapping over the top for which they would later achieve global renown. "I said, 'Do that. That's absolutely brilliant.' I thought the fast, punk-rock songs were so old-fashioned, like listening to The Depressions from 1976. That's why, when the album finally came out, the rap-rock songs were on Side 1, and all the fast punk-rock ones were on Side 2."

★   ★   ★

Following his stint with The Red Hot Chili Peppers, Andy Gill spent the mid-Eighties in LA producing bands and writing songs. There was talk of him making a record for ZTT, the label that brought the world Frankie Goes To Hollywood, Art Of Noise and Propaganda, and he recorded a solo single called 'Dispossession', which went some way towards getting the sort of sound he'd dreamed of achieving on Gang Of Four's last album, *Hard*.

Still in touch with Jon King throughout this post-split period, at some point in 1987 the pair decided to get together back in London, where they were both living, to work on some new songs. "We'd both gone off and done other things, so Gang Of Four wasn't the only life that we knew," says Gill. "The musical environment had changed in the USA, and we were continually being asked to do another Gang Of Four record. In 1988 we got excited about doing a record again."

A lot of the songwriting and programming of the beats was done in Gill's "fairly squalid flat" in Whitechapel, east London (he now lives in Holborn, in central London), with recording done using an eight-track machine. The idea was to combine the new computer technology with live guitars and drums. Several songs, among them 'Cadillac', 'Motel', 'Colour From The Tube', 'Everybody Wants To Come' and 'World Falls Apart', were written and recorded this way. Gill and King were also responsible for the artwork, including the cross-section of a brain and the ejaculating penis on the inner sleeve, a graphic depiction of the Ballardian lyrics of 'Everybody Wants To Come', with its images of "bodies at the side of the road".

The songs King and Gill worked on throughout 1987 and 1988 eventually became the album *Mall*, released by Polydor in 1991. Today, Gill is happy with the "amazing, clear-as-a-bell, chunky, big, fuck-off sound" of the record and the performances of the musicians, who included future David Bowie sidekick Gail Ann Dorsey and Dean (Curve) Garcia on bass, and ex-Haircut 100 sticksman Blair Cunningham on drums, although Gill concedes that, ultimately, Gang Of Four "are about playing live". *Mall*, eventually recorded in London and produced by Gill at the Maison Rouge, Power Plant and Strongroom studios during 1990-1, is an exemplary piece of studio product, with mixing and engineering courtesy of the likes of Jim Abbiss and Bob Kraushaar, and, according to Gill, some "amazingly clever beats and sounds ricocheting all over the place". That said, he considers it a strong return from the duo (only King and Gill appear on *Mall,* although Hugo Burnham and Sara Lee are thanked in the credits), with "really strong songs and some really fantastic lyrics", the exception being the cover version of Bob Marley's 'Soul Rebel', which he admits now was "a disastrous idea – if anybody else had done it, it would have been great. But it was not for us – it's just too beautiful and uncritical, you know?"

Following hot on the heels of the 1990 Warner Brothers release of a Gang Of Four collection entitled *A Brief History Of The Twentieth Century*, which featured liner notes by Greil Marcus and a mix of tracks covering the period from *Entertainment!* to *Hard*, *Mall* got mixed reviews. *Guitar Player* declared it "a stunning album recapturing the best aspects of the group's past incarnations", singling out 'Don't Fix What Ain't Broke' ("a driving dance anthem") and 'Satellite' ("an edgy but tuneful ballad"), and praising in general the album's commentaries on "communication problems, the Vietnam War, and the paradoxes of consumer culture". Dave Levesque of *Rhythm & News* called it "a thoroughly enjoyable piece of funk-drenched rock'n'roll." Elsewhere, there were positive remarks about 'Everybody Wants To Come' and 'Motel', which navigated the murky waters of voyeurism and sexual coercion, and 'F.M.U.S.A.' – an acronym for Fuck Me U.S.A., the slogan the prostitutes of Saigon wrote in lipstick across their semi-naked buttocks – which offered an alternate view of the Vietnam War: of the sexual-financial transaction between two of the main players in the Vietnam War, the black GI and the Vietnamese woman who, exploited within their respective societies, exploit each other in the violent, dislocated world in which they find themselves.

Around the turn of the decade, to promote *Mall*, a new version of Gang Of Four went on the road for dates in America with insurrectionary rap troupe Public Enemy and goth overlords The Sisters Of Mercy, which Gill found "a bit odd". *Variety* reviewed the GOF set, calling it "a pleasantly surprising mix of old and new", and noted that "Gang Of Four's socio-political point of view remains relevant some seven years after first breaking up." Even so, the low sales of *Mall* led Polygram to drop the group.

Session musician Gail Ann Dorsey already knew Andy Gill from when she was still living in Clapham, south London, and he had played guitar on the title track of her 1988 solo album for Warner Brothers, *The Corporate World*. "He wailed in with some of his fantastic guitar textures," she says from her home in Upstate New York. "He was just amazing – I love instrumentalists who have their own identity and unique sound. Anyway, a few years later Andy called me and asked if I wanted to work on *Mall,* and I ended up doing the tour as well."

She says she was more aware of Gang Of Four circa Sara Lee than the Dave Allen version of the band, and didn't really feel too au fait with their politically charged ideas, describing herself as "a closet, old school pop person" – she was most excited that the backing vocalists on *Mall* included Louise Goffin, daughter of Brill Building tunesmith-turned-counter-culture troubadour Carole King. In fact, it was Goffin who would later introduce Dorsey to Sara Lee, after which the two ex-GOF bassists embarked on a brief affair.

Dorsey says she considers Gill and King, then the Walter Becker and Donald Fagen of post-punk funk – a creative duo using hired studio hands – to have been terrific bosses. "They're just great characters, both of them, very intelligent, with a unique spin on things," she says, drawing the distinction between the more serious frontman and the guitarist with "the strange sense of humour" (she'd also met Hugo Burnham, describing him as "Mr. Nice, like a big, sweet bear"). She enjoyed the *Mall* sessions, particularly relishing the opportunity to sing with Goffin and rating highly the tracks 'Don't Fix What Ain't Broke' and 'Colour From The Tube', musically as well as lyrically.

"Jon's lyrics were incredible," she says, adding that the songwriter who most reminded her of King was David Byrne of Talking Heads, who also had an idiosyncratic view of American

society: "They're both witty yet deep and, you know, provocative."
She agrees with the Steely Dan comparison. "It seemed like it was
just the two of them, plus a great array of musicians," she says,
"although it definitely sounded cohesive, and it definitely sounded
like the Gang Of Four. Each player had their own identity and
style, but it didn't interfere with the entire piece." She was
impressed with Gill and King's rhythmic sensibility and can
appreciate what bands like the Chili Peppers see in Gang Of Four.
"I know Flea a little bit, and I know he adores the Gang Of Four
– they're one of the grooviest bands ever, always funky and 'in the
pocket'. They were incredible. Just about everybody I've played
with, when I tell them I was in Gang Of Four, they're like, 'You
played with the Gang Of Four? Wow!' Other musicians are always
really impressed. They're very well-respected and influential."

Dorsey fondly recalls the Public Enemy/Sisters Of Mercy/
Gang Of Four joint tour and remembers socialising with the band,
going to Gill's for meals, drinking with King, even a spot of
karaoke somewhere deep in middle America in a country &
western bar, where the black, shaven-haired Dorsey took it upon
herself to launch into a rendition of a number by cheesy c&w duo
The Judds. "Jon and Andy were cracking up at the back," she
laughs. "It brought the house down." Then there was the time she
hit King over the head with her bass guitar. "It was by accident,"
she explains. "You know how physical they used to get on stage.
One night, I remember him running across the stage, straight into
my bass. He was knocked flat out on the floor. I just thought, 'Oh
my God, I've killed him!' Luckily, he got up and started dancing
again." On another occasion, Gill ended up buying her a special
outfit. "Andy took me shopping in New York and he bought me
some black vinyl hot pants that zipped in half, so you'd put on one
leg at a time and zip from your ass straight around to the other end,
and a wig that made me look like Barbra Streisand in *Funny Girl*!
I was terribly thin then, and young and firm... It was this shop in
Manhattan where they sell all these trashy clothes – stuff for drag

queens. Andy made me wear them. He also bought me a pair of motorcycle boots. Not that I had a motorcycle…"

Finally, she remembers King on stage doing his unorchestrated manoeuvres in the semi-dark, the energy and intense volume of the band, the exhilarating crashing about that King and Gill would do, and the nightly ritual performed by Gill during which he'd smash up guitars. "He would have a box of new, cheap, 50-quid Strats that you could put back together and use again the next night. There would be three of four in a box every night, and he'd pull a new one out and crack it into a million pieces while Jon danced around. It was so exciting."

★ ★ ★

In 1992, towards the end of the US tours promoting *Mall*, Andy Gill and Jon King were offered the soundtrack for an intriguing film by writer/director Peter Hall, about an adolescent boy who murders his abusive father and gets away with it. At some point in the process of recording the soundtrack, it became clear that what they were working on was, in fact, destined to be another Gang Of Four album. That album turned out to be 1995's *Shrinkwrapped*.

"It remains one of my favourite Gang Of Four records, along with *Entertainment!* and *Solid Gold,*" says Gill, by implication acknowledging that, in retrospect, *Mall* didn't quite go according to plan. "This time, through bitter experience, we didn't let things through when we weren't entirely sure about them. We went over stuff again and again. We did a lot of it by fax. Jon would send some lyrics and I'd annotate them, line by line, what was good and what wasn't. We were really going to take the record to task, and I think that shows."

Shrinkwrapped, recorded, like its predecessor with a number of session players, received some accolades, even if it didn't exactly set the charts alight. Writing in *All Music Guide*, Jack Rabid noted that, "Singer Jon King and guitarist Andy Gill not only make up for that tepid album [*Mall*], but exorcise the lifeless ghost they left off with over a decade ago, *Hard*, and reclaim their spot as one of the most

original, subtly bracing, innovative, and unique bands around."
Among the excellent tracks on *Shrinkwrapped* were the hard-core
rocker 'Better Him Than Me', the robotic, narcissistic fantasy of 'I
Parade Myself' and album opener 'Tattoo', with its chilling depiction
of a serial killer using the language of love to seduce his victim:
"You don't know who I am/You don't know where I come from...
When you discover my name/I'll tattoo it on your heart." Then
there were the twinned 'Unburden' and 'Unburden Unbound'.

Gill explains the meaning behind the latter song(s). "'Unburden'
is me as a man in a motel room phoning a sex line and not quite
knowing what he's doing. He wants to talk to someone, and then
there's confusion between him and the woman he's talking to.
Masturbation is a secondary issue but the sex worker can only go
into her usual shtick, and the end result is a brick wall between
them. In the second song, Jon and I are talking about what we're
doing with that scenario." As with 'Anthrax' all the way back in
1978, from their debut EP, 'Unburden Unbound' saw Gill and King
splitting the screen and having a dialogue within the song. "I think
Jon and I always knew that our main strength as GOF was the way
everything we did emerged as the result of a dialogue between us,
and on both *Mall* and *Shrinkwrapped* that recognition took a more
concrete expression in songs like 'Unburden Unbound.' We realised
as the record took shape that there were various threads emerging:
onanism as a metonym for psycho-sexual dysfunctionality; people
growing ever more dependent on therapy and the parallel public
aspect of that Jerry Springer-style public therapy – that bizarre,
comic, emotional display on TV."

Two albums in four years? This was positively prolific for Gang
Of Four, especially considering they were meant to have split up a
decade earlier. Then again, as Gill says, "We never really planned
things, did we?" The material for *Shrinkwrapped*, at least at the
demo stage, was worked on this time at Gill's "swanky pad" by
Tower Bridge, in which the living room had been converted into
a studio, much to the delight of his new girlfriend, Catherine

Mayer, sister of TV comedy writer Lise Mayer, Angus Deayton's wife. "The whole thing was her idea, actually," says Gill, drolly, explaining that the idea this time was to make a record based less on samples and more designed for GOF at their most visceral and raw – on stage. It was also, albeit unintentionally and subconsciously, a reaction to the parochial, insular, nostalgic music then being made by the Britpop brigade, whose none-more-white beats and anaemic retro-pop were anathema to a band like GOF, who pioneered the idea of the funk-tional rock band. "We were very much aware of Blur and Oasis and we just thought, 'Why are they copying The Beatles so slavishly?' We were a bit mystified."

Despite the warm critical reception afforded *Shrinkwrapped*, and the slew of dates undertaken by Gill and King to promote it, soon afterwards the singer decided to get himself a full-time day job. Cue another hiatus for Gang Of Four. "We've always done Gang Of Four things because we've enjoyed it," says Gill, "and there's never been a grand plan, but that sort of put an end to Gang Of Four activities at that point."

★   ★   ★

One of the extra-curricular, non-Gang Of Four activities that Andy Gill busied himself with after *Shrinkwrapped* was the production of the debut solo album by former INXS frontman Michael Hutchence. Recording began in 1995 and continued throughout 1996 and 1997, during which period Gill also co-wrote some of the material alongside such other stellar collaborators as Tim Simenon of Bomb The Bass and Danny Saber from Black Grape. Work on the album continued right up until three days before Hutchence's controversy-riddled death in November 1997 from alleged auto-erotic asphyxiation, but didn't actually see a release until 1999, when it was largely overlooked due to lack of promotion by the label V2.

Hutchence had wanted to work with Gill because he had been such a great fan of Gang Of Four from right back at the inception of INXS, while Gill enjoyed Hutchence's music and company.

"He was a little bit shy," he says. "He wasn't massively imbued with over-confidence – it's a classic example of someone being the opposite of their stage persona, which was so much about bravado and swagger."

The pair first met in summer 1995, after which they became very close. "We were kind of best friends," says Gill. "Throughout that period we were working on stuff together on and off. Sometimes he'd go off and do a bit of INXS stuff, which he wasn't enjoying, but he'd taken a large wedge of advance – several million, I think it was – and he was trying to figure out whether he was going to give the money back or see through his commitment. But he wasn't particularly happy." It was through their working partnership that Hutchence, his partner Paula Yates, Gill and his wife Catherine Mayer, began regularly socialising together. "He and I and Paula and Catherine, we became a sort of unit. We'd go out together all the time."

This is possibly why Andy Gill and Catherine Mayer appeared over eight pages of the October 8, 1999 edition of celebrity gossip bible, *OK!*, on the occasion of their nuptials. It possibly also accounts for Hugo Burnham's strange outburst in chapter five of this book, in which the drummer makes angry references to, "Andy Gill, who's perpetually in the newspapers hanging out with rock stars and getting his face about with other famous people in *Hello!* or whatever that fucking magazine is."

"Yes, he was very bitter about that," says the guitarist. "It's completely due to jealousy, but it really gets Hugo's goat."

In the article, Gill and Mayer are photographed in full wedding regalia, surrounded by such small-screen entertainment luminaries as comedian David Baddiel, Gill's brother-in-law, Angus Deayton, his wife Lise Mayer, as well as the late Hutchence's other half, the troubled, notorious over-indulger Paula Yates, who was herself then less than a year from her death as a result of what the coroner would call "foolish and incautious behaviour".

Because of their closeness, Andy Gill and his new wife were chosen as godparents to Hutchence and Yates' baby daughter,

Heavenly Hiraani Tiger Lily Hutchence (known as Tiger), who was born in July 1996.

"Catherine Mayer and Andy Gill, the godparents of Michael Hutchence's daughter, join close friend Paula Yates to remember the INXS singer after their touching wedding ceremony," ran the caption to the main photograph of the feature. It was all a long way from 'Armalite Rifle' and gigs upstairs at the Fenton.

After Hutchence's death, Gill was approached by numerous tabloid reporters, wanting to get the scoop on the real reasons for the singer's death – was it really sex-related, or actually suicide? Gill refused to talk at the time but today says that he believes "it was a drug-related death. Simple as that." Of the period surrounding the death – and that of his other good friend Paula Yates, he says, "It was just dreadful." He adds: "When Michael died Paula went pretty much off the rails. She was so upset and sort of crazy, and although she'd never been a drinker, she was drinking and going bananas. I'd spent about four days in her hotel suite with her in Sydney for the funeral and immediately afterwards – her, baby Tiger, and me in this suite, with her on the 30th floor of this skyscraper hotel in Sydney, chucking CDs out the windows. I'd be telling her, 'Don't do that. You're going to kill someone.' There was a lot of looking after Paula at that time – Tiger too, although Catherine was more involved with that than me. We got her into the Priory [famous clinic for drug and drink-addled celebrities], which was a complete waste of space. I remember driving out there a couple of times thinking it was a bit of a joke. Well, it did a bit of good, just in the sense of keeping her out of trouble for a while. And you're not supposed to be able to have kids there with you, but we argued the case and they gave in, and so Tiger was in there with her.

"Anyway," he continues, "after about a year she'd calmed down and was making great progress and becoming much happier and more stable. So it was a great shame that what happened, happened [Yates died in September 2000, aged 41, from an accidental heroin overdose]. It was just a drug dealer popping round on the wrong day. A shock to the system? Yeah."

CHAPTER 10

RETURN THE GIFT

"You know that line from 'At Home He's A Tourist' – 'Two steps forward/Six steps back'? That's the story of Gang Of Four".
– Hugo Burnham

Even though they had split up 20 years earlier and the two albums subsequently recorded by Jon King and Andy Gill, *Mall* and *Shrinkwrapped*, had been released to little fanfare, in the early part of the 21st century Gang Of Four became *the* rock band name to drop in hip indie circles. It was like 1979 all over again, only this time this abrasive, angular noise, previously the preserve of the John Peel show, was all over daytime radio.

First it was American dance-rockers Radio 4 and The Rapture, and then the new British exponents of jerky indie-disco, Franz Ferdinand, Bloc Party, The Futureheads and the rest, who were transforming GOF's radical punk-funk experiments into accessible chart pop. Suddenly, after years of The Beatles and The Rolling Stones being the most namechecked white rock bands of them all, it was Gang Of Four's influence, their sound and vision, that could be detected everywhere. Suddenly, it made sense that the originals, the real McCoy, should come back to remind everyone where it all began. As one journalist wrote as news broke that Gang Of Four were coming back, "They continue to be the coolest band in the world as everyone cops their rhythms, guitar style and deliberately blank voices."

It was around 2004 that Dave Allen realised his old band's time had come again, when he took his 15-year-old son to see Franz Ferdinand in concert in Portland and mistook their song 'This Fire' for GOF's 'Damaged Goods', to the extent that he "thought they were taking the piss".

Andy Gill, who has produced at least two GOF fan bands in The Red Hot Chili Peppers and The Futureheads, says he knew "the awareness was always out there, but now it's reached critical mass", adding that "people have finally got tired of distorted grunge guitars and strange rock drumming". The guitarist has, over the years, grown accustomed to hearing snatches of GOF in other bands' music – including some of the biggest acts on the planet. "We got used to the Chili Peppers copying Gang Of Four, and there are some tracks that are like carbon copies of our sound, like their song 'Can't Stop' [from 2002's *By The Way* album]. You've got bits of Gang Of Four in U2, and you get quite a lot of Gang Of Four in R.E.M. Of the newer bands, I actually talked to Bloc Party about producing their first record. There was a point where everybody's lead guitar all sounded Gang Of Four-ish; even the beats were sort of Gang Of Four-ish."

This is why it made sense for the band to reconvene as they did in 2004. "I think it was something to do with it, yeah," agrees Gill. "There had been a few phone calls over the years. I think Dave had rung me up once or twice, and he came around here [to Gill's Holborn flat] in 2001, feeling me out about that sort of stuff, and every once in a while I'd get a phone call from him. Then it started to get a bit of momentum, and I thought, well, maybe we could [re-form]. One day I said to Jazz [Summers, of Big Life Management], 'I'm thinking about Gang Of Four doing something or other.' The words had no sooner left my mouth than he'd booked a rehearsal room, booked flights for Dave, everything."

As for Jon King, he says that he'd lost count over the last few years of the number of people "who have said to me, 'I heard a record that sounded exactly like you.'" He added: "It has gotten ridiculous. Even my daughter's gone, 'Daddy, is that you on the radio?'"

Actually, according to Allen, the band had already decided to get back together in their original configuration for the first time since his dramatic departure in 1981 by the time he went to see Franz Ferdinand perform live. "I actually went to the Franz Ferdinand show just to check them out, because there had been all this talk and bluster about how much like Gang Of Four they sounded," he says. "I really enjoyed the show, but I remained confused as to what everyone thinks is the connection. Other than some songs that have definite Andy Gill-type guitar riffs to them, I'd say there's not much else there. It's been a little bit of a lazy media angle. It's easy to drop names left, right and centre, whether it's Gang Of Four or XTC or whoever. If the journalists pulled out *Entertainment!* and gave it a really good pounding, and then put on one of these bands' albums, you could find out whether anything's similar there or not. To me, Franz sound more like Orange Juice, Josef K or Scars – you know, one of those early-Eighties Scottish indie bands."

For Allen, the biggest difference between GOF and the new generation of punk-funkers lay in the former's politicised lyrics. As he puts it, "Although we created a very original musical style, I don't think we'd be here today if it wasn't for our political stance. I don't see any bands out there today that can be compared to Gang Of Four. The new post-Gang Of Four bands aren't actually Gang Of Four-like: they want to be rock stars; they think politics is a bummer; there's no room for doubt. They just want to be consumed. Gang Of Four's music, and the post-punk art-music scene, was about being consumed.

"Rage Against The Machine were compared to us at one time, but hell, we never sounded like that," he continues. "Where Zack

[De la Rocha] was coming from lyrically was a way more personal and radical viewpoint than ours. So it was like, 'Why the hell are we being compared to them?' I think ultimately it might be because [guitarist] Tom Morello wore a beret with a red star on it, so it's like, 'Oh, cool, left-wing. They must sound like Gang Of Four.'"

Allen is similarly perplexed by the comparisons between GOF and US hardcore band Fugazi. "Fugazi were named as the next generation Gang Of Four but I think it was more about their attitude – 'We will not play any show for more than $5 tickets. We'll get the kids in. We'll play all ages, and we'll sell our albums as cheap as we can.' I think in journalists' minds it became, 'Oh, they're like the Gang Of Four', as in socialists or something. I don't think it was the money thing; it was just that they were anti-capitalist. And probably still are. And we were seen as anti-capitalist but we weren't, you know. In fact that's a distortion of what the real Gang Of Four were about."

Andy Gill concurred about this lack of either a political dimension or a "reckless, oppositional" stance when he said of the new breed, "The one thing that none of these bands have ever borrowed [from us] is the lyrical content – the ability to deconstruct the life we live and rebuild it and sing about it. Equally, these bands are just as conservative as the world that they're operating in." Asked why so few bands have ever gone as far as covering Gang Of Four, he replies with a question of his own: "Why bother when you can make a career out of sounding like us?" Next to Gang Of Four, considered Allen, the revivalists were mild, conservative and overly fashion-conscious. "They hardly break a sweat and look gorgeous in their clothes – that's not what Gang Of Four are about." Nevertheless, he conceded that the will to teach the new kids a lesson remained strong. "The goal is to be as incredibly intense as we were the first time around. What we have to do is leave them with their tongues hanging out again. If not, we don't retain our authority in the musical canon. There's no excuse that we're 23 years older." Jon King put it simplest when he referred to the young GOF-alikes stingingly as "collaborators".

All the more reason, then, for Gang Of Four to return and set the record straight about who they were and what they were about. "There was so much pressure from the outside that we all at least had to sit down and talk about it," says Allen. "It would have been stupid to say, 'Nah, can't be bothered.'" Best of all, for once all four members were in agreement about something. "Turned out there was genuine interest from all four members to perform again," he says, adding, "I was the first member of the band to leave and I never figured that I would be allowed to play with them again. This is like divorce central. And yet, I suppose things kinda just happen. Finally the planets were aligned and each member said, 'OK.' Even Dave," he laughs.

For Gill, it was the freshness of material a quarter of a century old that convinced him that re-forming was the right thing to do as much as the ubiquity of GOF's sound among the new indie fraternity. "The impetus for re-forming has a lot to do with current bands; that's quite a motivating force," he said in 2005. "But what's really exciting is playing these songs again. They sound like they could have been written two weeks ago. They sound like 'now'."

King, approaching 50 when the reunion was mooted, drolly suggested that he was initially interested by the possibility of getting sponsored by Stannah stairlifts "now that Thora Hird has died". He says, "The worst thing about getting old is catching a glimpse of yourself in the mirror. You've got food stains down your front, and wine, and you look like Sir Les Pattison. There I am thinking I'm this suave James Bond character, and there's Sir Les staring back at you." He only finally got the message when his 17-year-old daughter's friends turned up one day asking for autographs on the eve of GOF's prestigious London reunion show in 2005. "They'd all bought tickets to our London show not knowing that her dad was in the band!"

As for Hugo Burnham – who says he realised that "we could do it because we all still had our hair" – he expressed relief that he'd be able to supplement his college salary with some highly paid live work, even though it would mean having to interrupt rehearsals to fly home for the first week of term. The drummer said in 2005, "We got together last year. We thought, 'Yes, we can do this; it's a hell of a challenge but we can do it. We've got nothing to prove but it could be fun, so let's go for it.' We're all 48, 49 now and working like buggery. But I don't want to let the other three down. We were extraordinary once, and it has to sound extraordinary again. If we have fun together then everything else will fall in behind it." Referring to his weight and any middle-age spread he might now have, he said: "Yeah, I'm a fat bastard but I'm still a lot smaller than Frank Black, and everyone's loving him right now."

And so it was that, in late 2004, Gill, King, Burnham and Allen reunited for an extensive tour that would take them through England, leading towards a major outdoor performance at 2005's Coachella Valley Music & Arts Festival, America's premier summer rock showcase.

Burnham explains that he and Allen had been discussing the prospect of a reunion for a while. "Dave and I had been talking about it on and off for a long time, because we'd both been in and around the business, and it had often come up: 'Oh, you guys should get back together.' And then I think when the Pixies did it, we actually started getting calls, as did Andy Gill. And in the summer of 2004 I actually put in a call to Andrew, and he said, 'OK, fuck it, if Jon King wants to do it...'" King's demands were basic: "We agreed to play together again on one condition: we had to be great."

The drummer had, he says, been in irregular contact with Gill and King since quitting the band in the mid-Eighties. "I probably spoke to Andrew once every three years maybe. And I'd actually seen Jon once. And then, in our [Burnham and his wife] last year living in LA, Andy was in town and a mutual friend said, 'Oh, let's all go to dinner.' And I said, 'Yeah, and I'm bringing Dave Allen.'"

But Burnham believes there was a small matter for the bassist and the Gill/King axis to overcome: the "continued huge animosity" from King and Gill towards Allen, "because he left [the band in '81]."

Today, Gill denies that there were any hostile feelings towards Allen, either at the time of his departure from the band in 1981 or the reunion in 2004. And he points out that, although Allen might have felt ostracised from the rest of the group, the fact is he shared a room on that fateful US tour of 1981 with the guitarist and the pair were very close. "At that point in time I considered Dave to be a really good friend, and I was rooming with him all the time, so when he announced that he was leaving I was in shock. I knew he wasn't happy because we'd been sharing a room, and he'd be sitting in the dark, staring at the wall. And I was thinking, 'Something is fucking wrong here, he's not his usual chirpy self at all.' So when he said he had to go, I said, 'I wish you the best of luck and I hope everything turns out OK.' It wasn't the way Hugo's saying it, which is almost as if we were shouting at Dave or something, which we never did at all. I mean, privately, Jon and I were like, 'Fuck, he's really fucking dropped us in it.' But to him, we were completely wishing him well; both of us were totally kind."

The one thing that had annoyed Gill and King was the interview that Allen gave to *NME* after he'd left, in which he gave a new and unexpected reason for his departure. "We got pissed off when we came back to London [from the US tour] and found that Dave had done an interview saying the reason he left the band was that he didn't like Jon's politics – he implied that Jon wasn't left enough, which was just fucking bizarre – and that made Jon really angry, especially since Dave had been living in Jon's house in Muswell Hill. That did piss him off, which is fair enough, I think."

So what did it feel like when, in November 2004, these four often warring individuals finally found themselves in a room together for the first time in almost two and a half decades? Typically, they've all got their own take on that first meeting. "It feels great," said Dave Allen at the time. "It's interesting: I liken it to any team of people that operates together to get something done. There's always been that natural camaraderie, and that came back real quickly. Once we had our meetings and our discussions and aired some of our past grievances, we just got on with the job at hand, and I think everyone's been doing a stellar job. Clearly we're older and wiser, a lot more mature. We have a different world view these days and we're less likely to disagree and fight with each other." Contradicting himself somewhat, he later told this author, "We're in the room and there's Hugo and Andy and Jon – Jon was the last to arrive – and immediately I'm like, 'Fucking hell, we grow older but we never, ever change." Said Andy Gill, "You'd think after all this time there'd be hatchets to bury but it was really good to see everybody again. It was quite charming, actually. Same old humour, same old squabbles." Allen recalls the first reunion tiff. "After five minutes Hugo and Jon were at it. Hugo said something about the cost of a train ticket into London from Heathrow being £20 – 'That's about $40' – and Jon went, 'No, it's not'. 'YES, IT IS!' Then they were at it. Me and Andy were just looking at each other thinking, 'Christ! That didn't take long'."

Interviewed for this book in November 2007, Allen admitted he felt good about the way the initial meetings and the subsequent rehearsals went; even the sessions during which they worked on brand new material augured well, despite Burnham's doubts that audiences would be interested in hearing anything but classic tracks from the reunited Four. He was particularly pleased that their playfully frictional relationship was still intact. "We were in the studio yesterday – that's where you see the other side of Gang Of Four. We have always been incredibly, intelligently witty – we have the skills to find each others' weaknesses and exploit them and then laugh about them. That side of Gang Of Four has not been thoroughly documented. It's pretty amazing. I was rolling around yesterday about something somebody said about a TV show. We are the funniest band and we are the dourest band – you get both with us."

It wasn't long, however, before doubts began to be raised about Burnham's position in the re-formed Gang. Allen talked about the drummer being "serially unhappy about something that manifests itself in the band", despite the fact that, this time round, they were "getting paid more than we ever got before, and we're playing to bigger audiences." He added, "I, personally, am delighted." He talked about Burnham's tendency, as per the old days, towards "micromanaging" everyone and everything: "He started doing what he did the first time round, like trying to micromanage the manager, the tour manager... He'd be like, 'Give me the budget, cut that out so we can make more money.' It's like, 'Hugo, the world does not operate like this, especially the rock world. You start micromanaging the tour manager and the tour manager's going to complain to the roadies that you're a dick and you're not letting him do his job, and the roadies are not going to do their jobs because they're behind the tour manager because he's their boss... Eventually, the system starts to break down. So could you please shut up and get on with it.'"

Nagging doubts aside, the 2005 Gang Of Four shows were spectacularly well received, and the signs were that the re-formed unit could finally capitalise on their pioneering late-Seventies work. Dave Allen had promised on the eve of their comeback gigs, "Anyone coming to the shows will immediately see that we are light years ahead of [the new GOF-alike bands]. I've seen some of them live and they're just not a patch on Gang Of Four." Comparing the old and new versions of their classic songs, Andy Gill joked about "the skinny primitivism of the original text as against the muscular, beefy, luxuriant 2005 version".

Reviewers, awestruck by the newly galvanised and remarkably relevant GOF, gasped at the way Jon King "flailed and twitched, dropped to the floor and leaped up like a funky scarecrow, as hyperactive as he was a generation ago". King himself declared after the first shows, "It's the tragedy of old age that people stop doing stupid things. When you're young, you're reckless and oppositional, and that's what you should be your whole life. Why should you not take a risk?" Immediately reclaiming the immaculate ferocity that made them one of the signal post-punk bands, along with Joy Division, Wire and PiL, their unique blend of the cerebral and the visceral was in full force as King sang lyrics like, "Fornication makes you happy/No escape from society". At those initial comeback gigs, the singer pumped his hips, waved his hands in the air or simply stalked the stage, his long, Mao-like suit jacket half-unbuttoned as he Jesus-Christ-posed and crabwalked between three microphones, barking his words out. He even bashed a microwave during 'He'd Send In The Army' with a duct-taped aluminium bat, as the song stammered and surged around him. As the song finished, King knocked the microwave off its pedestal with a single stroke. Andy Gill sliced away at his guitar, familiar riffs shooting from the PA with the vitality of, as one writer described it, "sparks kicking off a welder's torch". During his own feedback showcase, 'Anthrax', he tossed his guitar around the stage, coaxing anguished howls from the machine.

Meanwhile, for the rhythm section it was minimalist business as usual, Allen positioning himself in front of Burnham's kit as the latter performed his tricky drum parts with a casual nonchalance. Most of the set at these reunion shows comprised tracks from the *Entertainment!* and *Solid Gold* albums, although 'I Parade Myself' (from 1995's *Shrinkwrapped*) got at least one airing, while 'To Hell With Poverty', was arguably the highlight of each performance. Prefaced by Gill's queasy string-bending, the funk-noir classic soon opened up into a monstrous groove, with King's echoed cries bouncing off the venue walls and setting into motion the crowd, who would mosh and crowd-surf as King flapped his arms, conducting the audience like they were his orchestra. No wonder, after one particular gig, a breathless young fan in his twenties was heard to sigh, "I hadn't realised how much all the bands I like sound like them."

Allen was as blown away by the crowd's reactions as the crowd were by the band. "It was insane, completely over the top," he says of audiences' responses to those 2005 gigs. "There was almost a sense of gratitude from the audience's point, like, 'Thank God, they're back.' I think there's been a definite longing for something this robust and this intense back on stage. Gang Of Four are all about the live shows ultimately. The albums are great and I would never downplay that, but I think live is where the experience truly lies.

"I'm 20 years older than I was, but I'm 100 per cent capable of playing the music identically," he reassured. "I'm in good shape personally and I've been playing all my life. The challenge was getting that chemistry back among all four people, and that came back really quickly. We're 20 years more experienced. I've got three kids, and when anyone has children, that creates a different vortex in your life, and you feed off that in different ways. I'm more confident and settled in myself. I'm also less insecure and don't feel the need to argue and fight for everything." The bassist believed this to have been the optimum moment for GOF's return, what with America "hell-bent on global hegemony" and their lyrics remaining "as important and relevant as they were back then, because not much has changed". He stressed that nostalgia had nothing to do with it. "None of us are looking back with our rose-coloured glasses on, trying to recreate what we were back then. We're not those people." On whether or not the band would play *Top Of The Pops* this time, he said, "Yeah. And if they tried to censor us again, then we'd walk off again. It doesn't matter. Our principles haven't changed."

★   ★   ★

When interviews began for this book in November 2007, everything looked rosy for the re-formed Gang Of Four.

Following those highly acclaimed 2005 shows and further foreign forays in 2006, Dave Allen, Hugo Burnham, Andy Gill and Jon King were all looking forward to finishing new material they'd been working on throughout 2007 for a brand new album – the first to feature the original four members of Gang Of Four since 1981's *Solid Gold*, making it almost as long a layoff as the one endured by such other comeback kids as The Stooges, New York Dolls and Big Star, whose recent albums were those legendary bands' first releases for 30 years or more.

But quite early on a rift opened up between Gill and King on one side and Burnham on the other, with Allen hovering somewhere in between. "I just thought, 'Wouldn't it be nice to get them in the same room without spitting daggers at each other?'" says Burnham. "And it was very cordial to start with – it was fantastic when the four of us were together on the road, on a stage, or in the rehearsal room; that was all beautiful. But the business side of things ruined it. You know that line from 'At Home He's A Tourist' – 'Two steps forward/Six steps back'? That's the story of Gang Of Four.

"I came over in 2004 for my parents' wedding anniversary and arranged to go for a drink with Andrew and Jon," he goes on. "And we talked about it and it was all very nice, but the two of them seemed wary about getting Dave involved. They were like, 'Well, not Dave, we can't have Dave, because he's too unreliable' – they'd heard stories about Dave quitting Shriekback the way he did Gang Of Four and I said, 'Dave did not leave in the middle of a tour or anything like that', which was a bit of a white lie because he did sort of dump Shriekback in the middle of a tour. I just said, 'If this is going to go forward we can't do the chicken in a basket circuit.' Then we talked about our failings from before and Jon said, 'Communication. We have to communicate properly this time.' That was where everything broke down: we didn't talk about things properly, and we didn't share what was going on, and I should have left it at, 'If it's not Dave, I don't want to do it,' because the only band anyone really wants to see is the original four. That's no diss to Sara Lee at all, but do you want to see The Who with Keith Moon or do you want to see them with Kenney Jones?"

Burnham was particularly unhappy about the lack of discussions with regard to the choice of Andy Gill's manager, Jazz Summers, to look after the reunited Four. "It was going to be Andrew's manager or not at all, which I wasn't very happy about because I hadn't met him. I'd heard a lot about him, and none of it was good, and to be honest, before long all my fears came true. Because the manager made lots of promises that he didn't fulfil. Jon said communication was crucial. Well, he [Summers] would not tell us anything. I felt like I was 23 again, living in a squat in Brixton just waiting to be given the call. It's like, we're fucking 50 years old; we've got families and real jobs. Give us a weekly phone call. 'This is what's going on. This is what's being planned. What do you think of this? What do you think of that?' Instead, he gave us these little secretary girls to look after us."

Burnham also points towards a series of what he calls "missed opportunities", including two "very high-paying, corporate-sponsorship gigs", that could have helped Gang Of Four build up the momentum achieved by the newly re-formed Pixies: one in New York at the Hard Rock Cafe, and the other at the South By Southwest festival in 2006.

"I'm not sure what Hugo means by 'missed opportunities'," interjects Gill, "because we did, in fact, do those two shows."

Nevertheless, it soon transpired that Burnham and Summers were not mutual fans. "His communication skills are horrible. And he just didn't like me. Andy Gill told me at one point, 'He hates it when you call him 'Dear Boy'. It's patronising.' I thought Andrew was taking the piss."

The piss-taking was rife, says the drummer. "Jon sent out an email just after we'd all got back from the first meeting, when we all had a drink and decided we were going to do it, making some sort of comment about 'the celebrity fat club', and I took offence because I thought, 'Oh, fuck it, here we go. We've barely started and he's calling me a fat cunt again.' I mean, I am a fat cunt but that's not the point. The only time the manager would talk to me it was like, 'Oh, the boys don't think you're up to it. Are you running? Are you rehearsing?' It was just this patronising, rude fucking tone from – and I'm quoting one of his peers here – this 'jumped-up bloody cab driver'. He was so mean."

More than anything, Burnham feels disappointment at the way things panned out considering how promisingly they began. At a "secret" early warm-up gig in a small pub down London's Old Kent Road, he remembers not being able to see the ceiling, so tightly packed in were the punters. Then they started playing and the past few decades just melted away. "At the end of the first song I just looked at Dave, and without sounding like a ponce, it was like a magic look between us, like, 'Fucking hell, we've just dropped 30 years off our lives.' It was every bit as good as before; better because we weren't actually high. It really felt like I'd gone back in time. Then I looked to the back of the room where I saw my 23-year-old nephew giving me the hairy eyeball, so that ruined that moment for me, you know, thinking I was 23 again. But it was magic, fantastic."

The band's triumphant performance at London's Shepherd's Bush Empire was a highlight. "It was so exciting because there were all the fat balding bastards like us, squeezing into that little jacket that's been hanging in the cupboard for 23 years. And there were all these young kids there, too, which was very encouraging. And it was great for Carol my wife and my daughter Tessie to see me do my thing. But some old problems came back, or never went away."

Backstage ructions at one gig on the comeback tour, in Bristol, ended with Burnham, head in hands, declaring, 'Oh God, it's all ending', and leaving the stage in tears. "I remember coming off stage crying, saying, 'This is it. I'm not doing any more of this.' Another time, we were playing in Austin, Texas, and Andrew screamed at all of us when we got off stage for letting him down by us playing badly and forgetting things. It was horrible. Another time, we had to pull over halfway to New York so that Andrew could give Dave a dressing down and tell him he had to apologise to the rest of us for fucking up the tour. That's how bad it is. The one who caused it will find fault everywhere else."

Andy Gill recalls the precise reason for this "dressing down": it was the fallout from a meal in a Philadelphia restaurant that resulted in a fight between himself and Allen. But it was not, as Burnham has suggested, a major altercation ending with "Dave going for Andy and everyone pulling him off". It turns out that one night, Gill's friend decided to take him and Allen, plus a pal of the bassist's, out for a meal to an expensive restaurant – "it must have been many hundreds of dollars" – during which Allen allegedly had a few drinks and "started ignoring us and just talking to his mate – he turned his back to us", says Gill. Apparently, at the end of the meal, "in a deliberate snub", Allen just "upped and walked out without a goodbye or a thank you – nothing at all. I couldn't believe it." At this point, Gill, feeling "really fucked off", left a message on Allen's mobile phone expressing his disdain for his behaviour. The bassist came to find Gill, who was standing on the pavement outside the restaurant. "So I walked up and repeated what I'd said on the phone message: 'What the fuck did you do that for? That was incredibly fucking rude.' And he hit me on the shoulder really hard and knocked me over onto the pavement, and that was that. I didn't respond. That was the full extent of it. There was no big fight."

Burnham is further aggrieved about the band's various travel arrangements, alleging that, "Andrew never wanted to go on the tour bus. He always wanted to fly – anything more than 100 miles – so that was more money for everyone to have to fork out, because he just didn't like to be on the bus." Gill dismisses this by saying, "That's totally untrue – if I flew and didn't fancy the drive, I paid for the flight myself."

Adds Burnham on a positive note, "When he's lovely, it's good to be around the four of us. But it goes back to the old days when he [Gill] was terribly mean to me, whether it was about my drumming or my weight. And I wasn't even fat back then! Or saying mean things about my dad… Why would he do that? Because he's a cunt. Not my dad – Andrew. He knows people's weaknesses and he goes for them."

Burnham even sees the 2005 *Return The Gift* album – a 2-CD package including one disc of re-recorded Gang Of Four classics and a second CD of remixes by GOF acolytes such as Yeah Yeah Yeahs, Hot Hot Heat and The Rakes – as another missed opportunity, because a) it was hardly promoted, and b) he feels that a band of the calibre of the Chili Peppers should have been invited to do a remix. In fact, as Gill points out, "Of course the Chilis were approached. But they turned it down because they were busy." Burnham is also unhappy about the cost of the record. "When we got the money from [record label] V2 to do the record, it was all going to cost 20 grand because Andrew was going to produce it himself at his studio, spending maybe 25 grand, and we'd all do it very well, thank you. Trouble is, he [Gill] is so slow. That was very frustrating. So the album ended up costing double what it should have done. It was very distressing."

As a riposte, Gill says: "It cost what it was supposed to: 25 grand. And Hugo got a quarter of the profits of the LP despite not playing a note." Countering Burnham's accusation that Michael Hutchence also found him slow to work with, Gill responds by saying that, "It was a really good partnership that extended beyond the recording studio. After all, me, [wife] Catherine, Paula [Yates] and Michael were practically inseparable till Michael's death. Plus, he asked me to be [Hutchence and Yates' daughter] Tiger's godfather, which I am. A lot of people who work with me want to socialise outside the studio and stay in touch years after projects are completed."

Burnham goes on to cite Gill's supposedly inebriated outbursts

on the occasion of the release of the 1998 Rhino 2-CD compilation, *100 Flowers Bloom,* as further evidence of Gill's allegedly
erratic behaviour. "When the guy at Rhino who was a friend of all
of us was putting together that album, he said he would have
Andrew calling him all hours of the night drunk, screaming that
he'd done a photo count of the booklet and there were too many
pictures of Hugo in it. As God is my witness, that's what happened.
He made the guy's life hell."

Gill has quite a different take on this incident. "I was
approached by Rhino to put that album together – the booklet,
the artwork, everything. I even label-managed it and chose the
track listing. I was totally responsible for all of it. So I put in a lot
of photos of me and Jon, believing as I do that that has always been
the core of the band. So anyway, the guy at Rhino called me saying
that Hugo and Dave wanted more photos of them in the booklet
– so it was actually the other way round to the way Hugo tells it.
I said no way; I wanted it the way I'd done it. But the bit about me
screaming at the bloke from Rhino down the phone is pure
fantasy on Hugo's part."

The last show of the re-formed Gang Of Four that Burnham
was involved in was at the end of 2006 in Somerset – in fact, he
"wasn't supposed to go" because the band had already been
rehearsing and writing new songs using a session drummer. "I
called Jon and said, 'You can't do a major show in England without
me. It's in fucking Somerset, 15 miles down the road from where
my family all live.' So Jon said, 'We've got to have Hugo on this.'
And it was like, 'All right, you can play that one, but then you go
home and we'll take the other drummer to Dublin the next day,
because we're doing all-new songs.' But they weren't – they didn't
have any new songs. It was all bollocks. After that, the manager
said, 'Fuck him – just get rid of him.'"

Burnham felt especially betrayed by Allen. "Even Dave Allen,
who wouldn't be there without me – he and I have been friends
for a very long time – started ignoring me and saying, 'I just can't

understand why you're angry all the time and you shouldn't have done this and you shouldn't have done that.' It's like, 'You cunt Dave, you were working harder than I was to get rid of Jazz.' Then Dave does this interview with *Billboard* online and says something about, 'Hugo's not with us at the moment due to undisclosed health problems.' I went fucking batshit, because you know what that means in the industry. The day after that appeared I had the head of HR at the college and the president's office call me and say, 'We need a word. Are you taking drugs? Do you have a drinking problem?' I emailed this to Dave. I said, 'Don't be a cunt. Don't say that.' Dave essentially accused me of making it up. It's like, no, here's the guy's name; he's head of HR at the college. I had to explain to my bosses on an alcohol- and drug-free campus that no, I did not have an alcohol or a drug problem."

The drummer blames the collapse of the reunited Four on "bad management", adding that it was a tremendous shame because "2005 was one of the greatest years ever of my life, because we got to show everybody not just how fucking good we used to be but that we were every bit as good almost 30 years on, despite being 100 pounds heavier." He was dismayed to read someone online saying that his second departure from the band was due to weight gain or a lack of professionalism on his part. "It's like, 'Screw you. Just don't even let anyone think that.' Because I was the only one who never made a mistake on stage, who was never too fucked up to play, or fell over because he was drunk on stage. I was fucking perfect, considering I hadn't played drums in 18 or 20 years; I was fucking brilliant. Anyone who saw it will tell you that.

"Listen," he adds, "I'm thrilled and we're very lucky to have had the chance to go back to it, and prove a lot of stuff to a lot of people, and the reputation remains untarnished, burnished even. It was the greatest thing to be able to go back there. And when the four of us were together, it was a laugh. In 2005, we were in Amsterdam, and we went out for a drink, just the four of us, no one else, and it was really heart-warming. Andrew, of course, will pooh-pooh and sneer at that because he's a cold motherfucker, but it was. We had a lovely time being around each other. And everything else notwithstanding, that was worth an enormous amount to me."

Finally, he assesses the relationship today between Gill and King. "Jon is the most well-spoken; a very smart man. But he's a bit bi-polar: he's loving and brilliant one minute, the next he's all sort of weird and cold and you can't get hold of him. But I think the tension and the stress are integral to our story. It is those four elements pulling in different directions at different times that made it so powerful. If everyone thinks the same, the art suffers. When it was just Andrew and Jon in charge of everything, that's when things got blanded out. But even Jon's had enough of Andy. At the end of 2006 he said, 'I'm fucking done with it. Andrew's such a miserable bastard. It's not fun any more.' But then that's the bi-polarity of Jon, because there he is back again doing it. They've had a very long relationship, but it's very tempestuous. Now they have nothing in common other than when they're doing Gang Of Four stuff. Jon hates being around him."

King is quick to contradict this latter assertion in the strongest possible terms. "That's absolute rubbish," he says. "Andy and I are as close as we ever were. It's just not true. I don't know where Hugo gets his insights from because he and I never talk. I've no idea. Andy and I work together very positively – we've been enjoying playing. In fact, since 2005 we must have played 70 shows, and we've never fallen out. There was a long period of time when we were pursuing our own careers, but… it's a mystery to me. We've had our ups and downs, but we get on fine! We're just a couple of blokes who make each other laugh. Our strange sense of humour sometimes careens into an area that makes us laugh collectively in a way that we wouldn't do on our own. Derek & Clive? There is a surreal element to it. Although it's probably more Baudrillard and Sartre."

"I've known Jon since 1970," adds Gill, "and immediately, when we got back in touch, we hit it off. A lot of it's about humour and shared interests. It's very difficult to work with each other this long, to be business-involved and be best friends, without falling out – that's quite a tall order."

"It's like a marriage," concludes King. "I doubt that there's a marriage where people haven't at some time or other disagreed or even argued about something or other. In fact, it almost defines human relationships. The only people who don't disagree about things are people that don't care about things or each other. I just don't understand it [Burnham's accusations]. We've been friends since we were 14."

★ ★ ★

"The problem with Hugo," says Andy Gill of the ongoing saga that is the Gang Of Four story, "is that, instead of playing or practising the drums, he always puts all his energy into trying to create wedges between me and Jon or to manipulate things behind the scenes. He won't take responsibility for anything that's not turned out right for him. In his mind, I'm the madly intelligent but totally evil ruler of a universe that he inhabits."

He describes an email sent in February 2008 by Burnham to Gill and King via Dave Allen as "like nothing I've ever seen before. He's capable of being very bitter and twisted. But one always wonders, 'What do you think you're going to achieve here? What's your ultimate aim? What's the positive result that will come out for you or anybody else?" Whatever the answers to those questions, one thing remains certain. "He's burned his bridges for good this time."

Gill disagrees with Burnham's contention that friction between the four members helped make them the creative force that they were. "I never bought into the idea that fighting makes good music," he says. "I've heard him say so many times that we were such different people and we should have never have met, but because we were different and because we fought, that created something that was angular and confrontational or whatever. But I really don't buy that at all. I think arguing is a waste of time. It's enormously energy-consuming, time-wasting and counterproductive. I've spent time with loads of groups, producing them, and it's always a bit of an eye-opener to discover that other people don't argue all the time."

He acknowledges that the Gang Of Four reunion hasn't quite gone according to plan, although it was a sketchy plan in the first place. "Nobody knew in 2005 when we got together to do this stuff quite what was going to happen. I think we all agreed to do some gigs, and they were fun, but then almost straightaway we started recording *Return The Gift*. By the start of 2006 we were talking about writing some brand new material, which Jon and I got dead excited about. But Hugo definitely made it very clear that he wasn't interested in doing new stuff. So, you know, you can't have it both ways."

One major issue for Burnham is that, financially, he's missing out. Says Gill: "He told Dave, 'Fucking Gill, fucking Jazz, ripping us off.' If he could just name one thing, one fucking taxi receipt too many...

"I'll tell you, on tour, we'd be going on a [internal US] trip, and we'd be flying from Dallas to Houston to Austin or wherever, and we'd be like, 'What the fuck is going on?' Because Hugo booked the flights in his role as micromanager, and it turns out he was just after the frequent flyer mileage so he could claim the frequent flyer miles for all four of our tickets. So we'd be flying all day when we could have flown direct; it would have taken an hour, but we'd have to fly all day. And he'd be sitting in Club Class while we were in economy. He'd say, 'Oh, I'll just use some of my mileage to upgrade myself on Eastern' or whatever the fuck the airline was, which none of us were members of anyway. We'd be sat there in economy while Hugo made us fly all around America when there was a convenient direct flight, and it would take all day – literally all day."

Burnham's response to this accusation that he was overly creative with America's internal flight system is full and frank. "Three times we flew indirectly on our second US tour – flights that I indeed booked. On one trip there was no choice as there were no direct flights with anybody, and the other two I chose Continental because they were the cheapest options. We're not the Pixies: our budgets were tight. Yes, I get flyer miles with Continental. No, I do not get flyer miles for other people – no airline does that, and if Andrew had a clue about touring other than constantly bitching about driving more than 100 miles a day on the bus, he'd know that. He'd also know that Eastern Airlines went bust about 20 years ago.

"On two legs I was upgraded because I have had a Continental Platinum Elite card for more than 10 years. Woo-hoo! I got a three-hour upgrade on a domestic flight – fucking luxury! That hardly compares with the Virgin Atlantic Upper Class upgrades from London to the US and back that [Jazz] Summers got Jon and Andy, while conveniently forgetting me on the same airline. Oh, and of all the trips to Logan/Boston airport and back during those two years, my wife drove me out once, and was able to meet me on the return a couple of times. I got receipts for a tank of petrol for her each time. Some rip-off. She has a full-time job and we have a child – two things Andrew has little concept of – so being my chauffeur really is not what she spent all her time doing. Every other time I took a car service from my house in Gloucester, 48 miles from Boston. The charge – on my Amex card – was between $85 and $95 each way. I gave the receipts in. Is it that big a deal?

"Andrew has a penchant for being rude about and to me – he always did. He likes his drummers to know their place."

And yet Gill doesn't accept that Burnham was ousted by the others in 2007, or even fired, simply because the idea in the first place was for it to be a temporary, short-term, part-time commitment from a full-time teacher with plans to study for a PhD and with no enthusiasm for new material.

Then again, the point is now moot because, on May 7, 2008, there appeared via email this statement from not just Hugo Burnham but Dave Allen as well. "For immediate release," it read. "GANG OF FOUR MINUS TWO. ORIGINAL RHYTHM SECTION ALLEN AND BURNHAM DEPART." It continued: "The original and best-loved line-up of famed post-punk icons Gang Of Four reunited in 2005 to great acclaim and success – but are no longer. Bassist Dave Allen and drummer Hugo Burnham are moving on, while singer Jon King and guitar player Andy Gill will continue, focusing on writing and recording new Gang Of Four music. Burnham last performed with the band at All Tomorrow's Parties in the UK in December 2006, while Allen played a few shows alongside a session drummer in 2007, and recently worked on new material with King and Gill. Allen says, 'At the beginning of April, I decided that I could no longer continue to be a member of Gang Of Four. My ability to give 100% to the band is limited and I feel that if I can't do so, then I shouldn't continue. As I expand my research and thinking about contemporary music distribution on Pampelmoose.com [Allen's popular blog], and as I focus on online technology and social networking at Nemo Design here in Portland, I find myself conflicted about how the band's new music should be released. To retain any credibility for Pampelmoose.com about what the future of music distribution will look like, I have to move on and not hold back Jon and Andy's music plans. I have had a side project for a while now with John Askew of Tracker and Menomena's drummer Danny Stein called Faux Hoax [pronounced Folks], and I look forward to fun times finding ways to get our music into peoples' hands in unique ways.' Burnham writes, 'It was a great couple of years of intermittently reminding people old and new, far and wide just how powerful the original four of us were together. Age only increased our power and focus on stage, and it was a rare pleasure to work with the original band once again. Being in a band requires handling the business side of it too, which

191

was boring, and the constant travel away from home became debilitating. I plan to start my doctorate, as well as broadening my teaching at more than one college here in Massachusetts, so my free time has become increasingly limited, making it difficult to be involved with them going forward. Musically, I am recording and writing with members of Boston noise-merchants, The Bags, and I have also been doing some recording lately with Mike Watt. I wish Jon and Andy luck with their new musical endeavours; I am sure they will be interesting."'

★   ★   ★

On May 9 and 10, 2008, Andy Gill, Jon King, bassist Thomas McNiece, of a band called El Presidente, and long-serving GOF drummer Mark Heaney played two gigs in Zagreb and Belgrade, the first time Gang Of Four had played in the region since 1981, when *Solid Gold* reached number one in Yugoslavia and, instead of the 300 or so punters they were expecting, 9,000 fans turned up. The 2008 shows were no less memorable and ecstatic. "It was," says Gill, "an incredible experience. The crowd were totally OTT. It was quite touching. They were screaming – it was like the peak of Beatlemania. After three encores, the road crew started taking our gear down, but the 2,500-strong crowd just refused to go anywhere, so after a while the crew put the gear back and we went back on stage for more. I told the audience it was our first show there for 27 years and that we had a special bond with the people of Zagreb. That took the roof off."

King was equally bowled over by the response of the audience in Croatia. "We hadn't played there since 1981 and that show was one of the three most significant we ever played," he says. "It assumed legendary proportions. Somehow we became emotionally one with the audience. Our gig in Seattle after Dave left the band was another – the one when Busta Jones joined and we were thinking of going home, and he learned the show in 24 hours."

Gill also remembers that fateful night. "We started playing and there was this incredible feeling that we'd transcended this bloody problem. The audience got it as well. It was transcendental."

"We had no idea that *Solid Gold* was such a huge-selling record over there," King returns to his Croatian reminiscence. "But this time, mirroring 1981, Dave for professional and family reasons decided to leave and we had another bass player [McNiece] who'd learned the set in short order. So there was a lot of anxiety and edginess among us all – would it work? Would the audience get it? And again we went on stage and the show was transcendental. It was one of those gigs where you wonder if you're playing the audience or the audience is playing you. We did two encores and our crew started breaking the equipment down; after 10 minutes it was still really noisy – no one had left the building, so we went back on stage. It was very emotional and intense: when it gels, audiences become transported by it and we get transported by the audiences."

At the time of writing – mid-May 2008 – Andy Gill and Jon King are still very much involved in writing and rehearsing as Gang Of Four, preparing for their performance at the summer's Massive Attack-curated Meltdown Festival and considering how best to deliver their new material in this download, cyber age. One idea is to record a brand new track every month and put it online as soon as it's ready, each one with a completely different producer at the helm – names being discussed range from indie sound whiz *du jour* Paul Epworth to electronica loon Aphex Twin. Gill says the new material harks back to the glory days of *Entertainment!* and *Solid Gold*, with the emphasis on the latter's sound, which the guitarist/producer has always considered to be "darker, murkier and more sinuous" than the "brightly lit" debut. He reveals that, just as he didn't really check out the competition prior to recording the *Damaged Goods* EP, he's not really investigating the new groups today. "I'm not much of a radio listener," he says. "I hear what comes my way, but I don't particularly seek stuff out. I just follow what's an interesting idea in my head."

He offers as example a song he's currently working on featuring two characters: "one from the 17th century who talks in a 17th century way, and the other from now." He believes the new songs will, broadly speaking, be in the vein of classic Gang Of Four material, musically and lyrically, because that's what bands tend to do – spend their "career" mining their particular seam of ideas. "I feel like the same person that I was when *Entertainment!* was done, and I get excited by the same ideas," he says.

King is especially pleased with a new song called 'Second Life', which references a recent Internet phenomenon involving a virtual world that enables users to live a completely separate, albeit virtual, existence. "The hook is the story of a pub-crawl night out in Soho," explains the lyricist. "That leads into the alter ego idea – that online world where people can become anything from a penguin to a super-capitalist."

"It's massive online," says Gill. "My missus was quite obsessional about it – she'd get up at 5am every day to do it. She got bullied by gangs of cyber hoodies in there and at one point she became a pole dancer and built a house!"

King was drawn to the Second Life site because it reminded him of the ideas he was exploring with Gang Of Four at the very beginning: "The idea of 'Second Life' is interesting – what the situationists talked about, what most influenced my lyric writing, was this idea that you live in this society where you live your lives by proxy and invest things that you see with all of these emotional values that you can't participate in: the Society of the Spectacle, they called it. Second Life is itself a spectacle: it's not real but it's actually more real than being real. You participate in life through a glass, darkly.

"In real life," he continues, "we end up having these detached relationships with our own existence and designate certain things as play activities that are highly controlled and constrained and delivered. People freak out about binge drinking, but it's a socially recognised way of letting off steam. In Japan, being drunk is an absolutely respectable way of behaving that says, 'I am now allowed a degree of informality in this strict society.' Lacan [20th-century French philosopher] said we construct a whole series of barriers and restrictions to something honest and true about ourselves. We allow ourselves to do some things and not others. The lyric to 'Second Life' goes: 'I'm in a French house and we're drinking halves/Girls with photocopies of their arse.' These days, we're 'allowed' to have these weird, psycho, office party things where people start snogging their bosses. It's like The Lord of Misrule in the Middle Ages – suddenly you can be queen for the day. You end up participating in your own misery."

"It's a parallel to your life where you think you've got the control – you've got the keyboard – but then a bunch of hoodies come along and mug you!" says Gill of secondlife.com. But the pleasures to be had from having a second life are deceptive. "There's a bit in the song where I sing about being out on that pub crawl, and I go, 'Hey! I'm running a tab! It's in my name!' At that moment everything's right with the world: you've got money, you're in control, you're with your mates. Then you get a glimpse of yourself and it's actually the opposite of that."

King mentions another new GOF song, tentatively titled 'American Man', emphasising the importance of the attention-grabbing opening line, citing two great examples as Rod Stewart's 'Maggie May' ("Wake up, Maggie, I think I've got something to say to you") and Blondie's 'Hanging On The Telephone' ("I'm in the phone booth, it's the one across the hall/If you don't answer I'll just ring it off the wall") – opening lines that "put you into the situation immediately, so you immediately know where you are".

Does King feel that he's still trying to resolve issues that he started wrestling with in his late teens and early twenties? "At the risk of sounding extremely pretentious," he replies, "Paul Cézanne painted the Mont Sainte-Victoire about a thousand times, over and over again. I was in an exhibition of his work and I stood next to these US tourists who were saying, 'Why did he paint the mountain so many times?' I found that when we got back together in 2005 I had to listen to the old stuff from *Entertainment!* and *Solid Gold* and *Songs Of The Free*. And I wondered what this bloke – i.e. me – was like, and I was really pleased to meet him. Whoever I was or we were, we were quite funny from my perspective. I very much enjoyed the ideas. And having immersed myself in those songs again – because I never listen to my own stuff once it's finished – it occurred, God, these are quite good ideas. We do live in a society of the spectacle, we do live our lives by proxy; the world of celebrity is real. There may be oil under Rockall [a reference to the lyrics of 'Ether' from *Entertainment!*]. People do invade countries in the Middle East for economic reasons. Those aren't nostalgic themes; they're real, modern and intense. To me, *Entertainment!* says quite a lot about late-Noughties Britain. It's not social reportage but it says a lot about being alive now, because if anything it's more relevant. I'm sure that's why our fans and other musicians get it.

"Modern music astounds me," he says, disappointed at the lack of political engagement among young musicians. "In the Sixties everyone during Vietnam, from Edwyn Starr to Kenny Rogers, would write songs about the war. Even 'Dancing In The Streets'. There's not one song today by any of the so-called radical indie rock bands about Iraq. I find it deeply confusing that people don't want to be engaged in other stuff. I love the Kooks and Klaxons and Amy Winehouse and Duffy's 'Warwick Avenue', but that sort of stuff could have been done at any time over the last 30 years. There's all sorts of horrible shit going on, and all sorts of fun shit, but no one's engaged with it."

Surveying the last 30 years as guitarist, producer and sometime singer with Gang Of Four (and, briefly, lover of Ian Curtis' bereaved girlfriend, Annik Honore), how does it all look to Andy Gill now? "That's a big question," he replies. "As you go along you don't know where it's going, do you? You don't look beyond next week, really, and you really don't even know what might happen then. Of course, in hindsight you can see how one thing leads to another, and I do feel lucky that I had the chance and the opportunity to use my imagination and do something that has been really interesting. I feel very lucky about that."

Does he agree that Gang Of Four enjoyed an early golden age that they failed to truly exploit? "Well, we've got a long history, and looking back over it all you can identify the things that were great and the things that were not so great," he says. "With a lot of artists, you can say they had a golden period at a certain point in time, and then it's arguable whether they ever captured people's imagination in quite the same way again."

Whether they could have been as big as U2, bestriding the Earth like four punk-funk colossi, is debatable. The fact is, Gang Of Four made their mark, made music to please themselves, made some records that have entered the pantheon, and made it possible for some of the biggest and most significant bands on the planet to exist. It's quite an achievement.

"At the very beginning you're not quite sure which way things are going to go. Some of the very first songs that we did, were just jokes," Gill says. "But then it starts to kind of crystallise into an idea and gains a little bit of momentum. And then you start to see where it could go; then it gets serious. That's when it's really worth working your ass off: it's worth getting that drum groove – you know, 'come what may we've got to get that drum groove' – because at a certain point, when it gets past critical mass, you know you've got to make it happen. Because you can see it; you can see what you can have. Hopefully, in time, you've done the hard work. You've created a playground for yourself that you can then occupy and continue to explore."

And how would King assess the value, achievement, impact, continued relevance and resonance of Gang Of Four today? "Recently, this journalist asked me, 'What do you think about being seen as a political band?' And I didn't know what to say except that the particular subject matter, what we do – not just the lyrics but also Andy's guitar and the way we've always approached things – to me it sounds like it's been dropped from outer space. It doesn't sound like anything else. We might have listened to Funkadelic but we don't sound like them; I love Chic's music but we sound nothing like them either. I think we have engaged in an approach that is very individual, one that I know has inspired many musicians, and that's one measure of our achievement. The guy from Ministry [Al Jourgensen] said they wouldn't have existed without us; Michael Stipe is a great fan, as are Bono and Flea from the Chili Peppers. And today there are fantastic bands like Franz and Bloc Party who have namechecked us. That makes me immensely proud, even if, commercially, we'll never be an act to challenge Amy Winehouse in the charts."

Gill sums up Gang Of Four's achievement like this: "We've married an incredibly insightful lyrical approach about the world around us that is funny and clever and true, with a completely original musical approach, and the two things are locked together; they're hand in glove. Then there's the thing about the drums and the bass and the vocals and the guitar all having equal space in the mix, not in a pyramid of importance but side by side. That's what makes the music incredibly fresh to this day and sets us apart."

Gang Of Four were never rock rebels, positing fighting in the street. It was a different kind of rebellion and agitation at the state of things. They were pointing out the inconsistencies while confirming that life is too complex to offer simple solutions.

"A lot of it is about the complexity of your relationship with the rest of the world around you," says Gill. "It's not simple, and it can't be described in the way that someone like Billy Bragg describes it. It's a complex relationship, and that's why Jon and I often take different positions in our songs. We don't, for example, have a simple relationship to money or banks – you think your money is just in a bank, but really it's being used to fund arms in Angola."

For Gill, this is why The Clash were easy to sell: because it was a simple "us versus them" proposition, whereas with Gang Of Four it was less clear-cut who "the enemy" were. "Totally," he says, finally. "It would have been easy to wave a red flag, to adopt a stance, to put one foot on the monitors and man the barricades. We could have done that, and the crowd would have loved it. But we don't feel that that's accurate. A lot of the time we're describing ourselves as being WITH the enemy. We're complicit. We're collaborators. It's not a straightforward world, that's what we think. And that's why our new songs, like our old ones, continue to pursue the idea that life is complicated and that there are no easy solutions to things."

ACKNOWLEDGMENTS

Paul Lester would like to take the opportunity to thank the following people he interviewed for this book, without whom it would not have been possible to tell the story: Andy Gill, Jon King, Dave Allen, Hugo Burnham, Rob Warr, Bob Last, Greil Marcus, Nick Launay, Chris Briggs, Sara Lee and Gail Ann Dorsey. Paul would like to stress how grateful he is for the involvement of the original four Gang Of Four members, who were cooperative and candid above and beyond the call of duty, especially Andy Gill, with whom the author spent so much time between November 2007 and May 2008 that he may as well have rented his spare room.

In addition, Paul would like to thank for their support, encouragement and inspiration during the research and writing of this book the following: Simon Goddard, Jon Wilde, Chris Roberts and Simon Reynolds.

And a special mention for his patience and guidance throughout the whole process to Chris Charlesworth of Omnibus Press.

ALBUMS DISCOGRAPHY

ENTERTAINMENT! (1979)
Ether, Natural's Not In It, Not Great Men, Damaged Goods, Return The Gift, Guns Before Butter, I Found That Essence Rare, Glass, Contract, At Home He's a Tourist, 5.45, Anthrax

SOLID GOLD (1981)
Paralysed, What We All Want, Why Theory?, If I Could Keep It for Myself, Outside The Trains Don't Run On Time, Cheeseburger, The Republic, In The Ditch, A Hole In The Wallet, He'd Send In The Army

SONGS OF THE FREE (1982)
Call Me Up, I Love A Man In Uniform, We Live As We Dream, Alone, It Is Not Enough, Life! It's A Shame, I Will Be A Good Boy, The History Of The World, Muscle For Brains, Of The Instant

HARD (1983)
Is It Love, I Fled, Silver Lining, Woman Town, A Man With A Good Car, It Don't Matter, Arabic, A Piece Of My Heart, Independence

MALL (1991)
Cadillac, Motel, Satellite, F.M.U.S.A., Don't Fix What Ain't Broke,

Impossible, Money Talks, Soul Rebel, Hiromi & Stan Talk, Colour From The Tube, Hey Yeah, Everybody Wants To Come, World Falls Apart

SHRINKWRAPPED (1995)

Tattoo, Sleepwalker, I Parade Myself, Unburden, Better Him Than Me, Something 99, Showtime, Valentine, Unburden Unbound, The Dark Ride, I Absolve You, Shrinkwrapped